Haunted Hi...

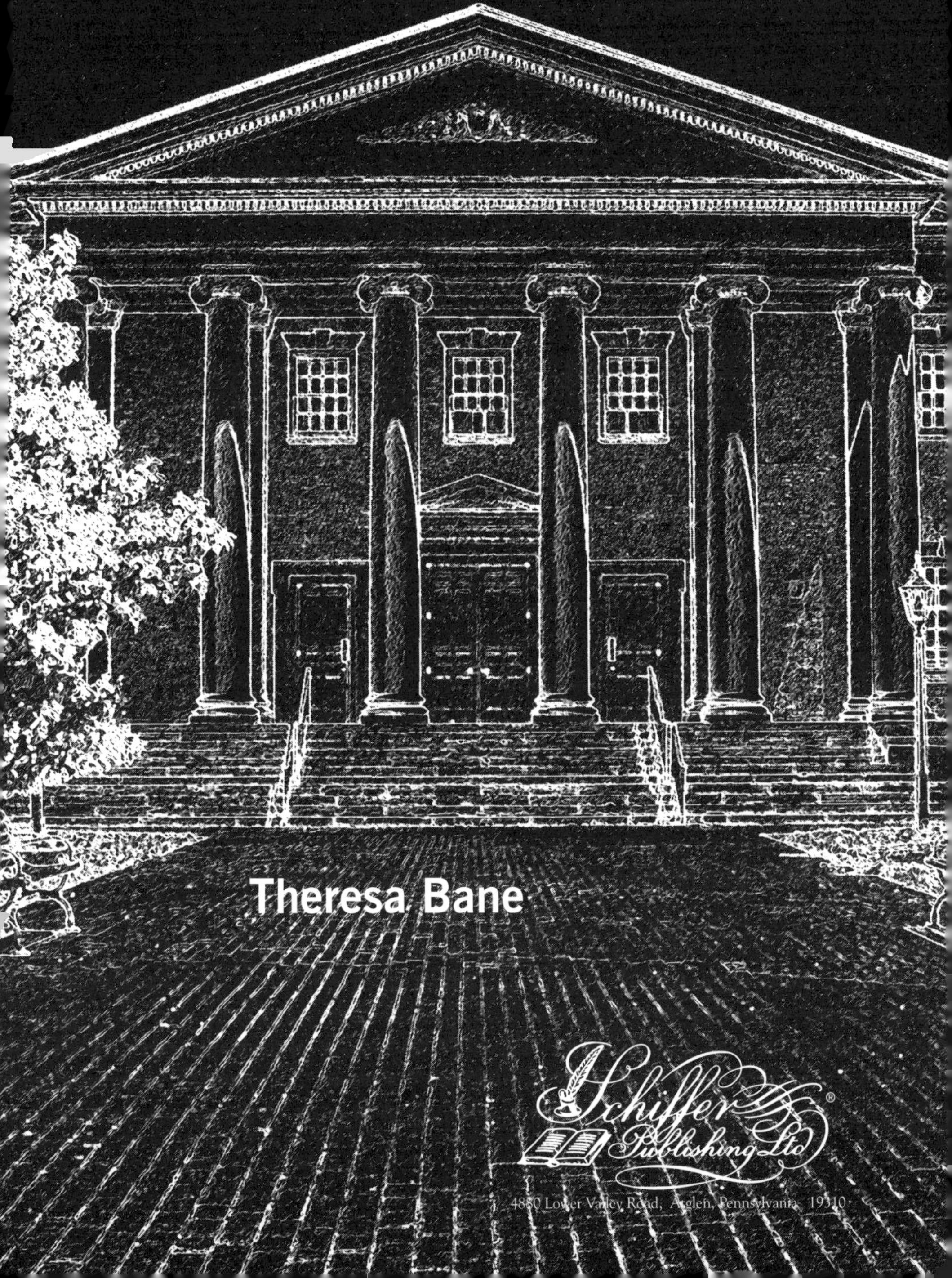

Theresa Bane

4880 Lower Valley Road, Atglen, Pennsylvania 19310

Other Schiffer Books on Related Subjects:

Civil War Tours of the Low Country: Beaufort, Hilton Head, & Bluffton, South Carolina,
   978-0-7643-2790-2, $16.99
Greetings from Charleston,
   0-7643-2488-8, $24.95

Schiffer Books are available at special discounts for bulk purchases for sales promotions or premiums. Special editions, including personalized covers, corporate imprints, and excerpts can be created in large quantities for special needs. For more information contact the publisher:

Schiffer Publishing Ltd.
4880 Lower Valley Road
Atglen, PA 19310
Phone: (610) 593-1777; Fax: (610) 593-2002
E-mail: Info@schifferbooks.com

For the largest selection of fine reference books on this and related subjects, please visit our web site at: **www.schifferbooks.com**. We are always looking for people to write books on new and related subjects. If you have an idea for a book please contact us at the above address.

This book may be purchased from the publisher. Include $5.00 for shipping. Please try your bookstore first. You may write for a free catalog.

In Europe, Schiffer books are distributed by
Bushwood Books
6 Marksbury Ave.
Kew Gardens
Surrey TW9 4JF England
Phone: 44 (0) 20 8392-8585; Fax: 44 (0) 20 8392-9876
E-mail: info@bushwoodbooks.co.uk
Website: www.bushwoodbooks.co.uk
Free postage in the U.K., Europe; air mail at cost.

Copyright © 2009 by Theresa Bane
Library of Congress Control Number: 2008941378

All rights reserved. No part of this work may be reproduced or used in any form or by any means—graphic, electronic, or mechanical, including photocopying or information storage and retrieval systems—without written permission from the publisher.
The scanning, uploading and distribution of this book or any part thereof via the Internet or via any other means without the permission of the publisher is illegal and punishable by law. Please purchase only authorized editions and do not participate in or encourage the electronic piracy of copyrighted materials.
"Schiffer," "Schiffer Publishing Ltd. & Design," and the "Design of pen and ink well" are registered trademarks of Schiffer Publishing Ltd.

Designed by Stephanie Daugherty
Type set in Bard/NewsGoth BT
ISBN: 978-0-7643-3174-9
Printed in United States of America

Dedication

This book is dedicated to my mommy,

Joan Falcone,

who not only taught me how to read,

but how to love books.

Acknowledgments

I would just like to say thank you to everyone who helped me out with the book. There are too many of you to even attempt to name, but a very special "thank you" needs to go out to these folks:

- General Manager of the Biltmore Hotel, Mr. Ronnie Dennison;
- Director of Blandwood Plantation, Ms. Ashlee Crayton Poteat;
- Photographer Karl S. Farargo;
- Historian and tour guide for the Carolina Theatre, Mr. Jeffrey P. "JP" Swisher;
- Public Safety Officer of Dana Auditorium, Rhonda Johnson;
- Section Chief of the NCDA, Dr. Colleen Hudak-Wise, Section Chief-Soil Testing NCDA&CS Agronomic Division, Dr. David Hardy, and Regional Soil Sample Scientist with the NCDENR, Mr. Perry Wyatt, retired;
- Historian and Park Ranger at the Guilford Courthouse National Military Park, Mr. John Durham;
- Director of Mendenhall Plantation, Ms. Rebecca Lasley;
- Masseuse and Massage Therapist at Salon Blu', "Rebecca";
- Owner and operator of the Twin Lakes Lodge, Mrs. Anita Gill;
- The Storyteller of the City of Greensboro, Mrs. Cynthia Moore Brown; and the City of Greensboro;
- For providing ghost stories and histories, thanks goes also to: Mr. James Fulbright, Mr. Richard Welborn, Ms. Mary Best, and Mr. J. Scott;
- Beta reader and quick edit queen, Mrs. Gina Farargo
- New best friend and editor, Dinah Roseberry
- My husband, T. Glenn Bane for all his support in my endeavors;
- And my ever-faithful assistant, Ms. Joy Poger, also known affectionately as Skuttles

Contents

Preface: A Word from Scuttles 6
Introduction: Gateway City and Ghost Vortex 8
Chapter One: Welcome to Greensboro, North Carolina 11
Chapter Two: Aycock Auditorium 22
Chapter Three: Biltmore Hotel 28
Chapter Four: Blandwood Plantation 41
Chapter Five: Carolina Theatre 48
Chapter Six: Cedar Street 61
Chapter Seven: Chestnut Street 64
Chapter Eight: Copper Creek & Deep River Mine Shaft 67
Chapter Nine: Dana Auditorium 70
Chapter Ten: The Devil's Tramping Ground 75
Chapter Eleven: West Friendly Avenue 93
Chapter Twelve: Guilford Courthouse National Military Park 97
Chapter Thirteen: Lydia's Bridge 109
Chapter Fourteen: Mendenhall Plantation 123
Chapter Fifteen: Purgatory Mountain 129
Chapter Sixteen: Richfield Road 135
Chapter Seventeen: Salon Blu' 140
Chapter Eighteen: Twin Lakes Lodge 145
Chapter Nineteen: Vampire Beast of Greensboro 152
Conclusion 157
Index 158

Preface

A Word from Skuttles

> If John Edward is a fake and knows it, he is a con artist.
> If John Edward is a fake and doesn't know it, he is delusional.
> If John Edward is not a fake, he is using his power for a sideshow,
> rather than providing evidence of the paranormal
> and ushering in a new era of discovery for all mankind to enjoy.
> At best I would call that irresponsible.
> *-- Alexander Poger (1966–2005)*

Moving from my home state of New York to North Carolina has had its challenges for me. We New Yorkers have a tendency to feel all things New York or New York related are just a little bit better than everything else. I hate to admit it, but I too once had the classic snark, which implies "all things from New York are better than anywhere else except maybe California." I spent loads of time with family in North Carolina seeking familiar things that I thought would provide comfort, like New York style pizza, bagels, mass transit, and museums. Most of all however, I missed my New York friends.

Shortly after my arrival in North Carolina I met an author named Theresa "Terry" Bane who asked me on a lark if I would join her one day on a ghost hunting excursion. I took my skeptic self, complete with a New York attitude, and went along—after all, how fun can a haunted *anything* be outside of wonderful New York? My little ghost hunting outing and fact-finding trips with Terry helped me come out of my grey New York cocoon and realize all the color and beauty that North Carolina has to offer, in particular the Greensboro Triad area. It has a rich history, culture, and aesthetic beauty that can only be appreciated in person.

A Word from Scuttles

I found Terry to be a truly impressive individual. She is relentless in seeking the truth, researching and testing theories. Often I found myself delving deeply into the research with her, scouring through death records, testing paranormal theories, interviewing every one associated with a story, checking endless reels of microfiche newspaper articles, and becoming good friends with the local librarians. (By the way, librarians are truly America's most underused source of knowledge.)

Terry is one of the most caring, humorous, and quick witted persons I have ever known. Often eyewitnesses were a little unsure if they should divulge information. They seemed at first concerned that Terry may make fun of, scorn, or not take them seriously. However, through her easygoing manner, humor, and professionalism she'd quickly and always put the interviewee (and I even think in some cases ghostly apparitions) at ease. In each ghost hunting expedition, it was only a matter of time before Terry got a person talking. If you ever meet her in person, offer to buy her a cup of coffee if she'll share some of her stories with you. It will be well worth the price of a Starbucks latte at the very least.

Ghost hunting, tracking, and research is so much better in person than what one may see on popular TV shows these days. I found myself in places I thought I would never go, and speaking with people who were absorbing and captivating. You can never tell just by looking at a person the secrets that they hold inside. I was on secluded roads, under bridges, jumping fences, and getting behind-the-scenes tours of so many historic locations. I never knew that the Triad has so much to offer.

I am fortunate that I was able to, for the most part, hang back and just "enjoy" the hunt. I was not held accountable to deadlines or publishers and was simply able to take pleasure in the experience. I learned that people here in the Triad truly love their heritage and are rightfully proud of it.

At the start of this great adventure, I was a die-hard skeptic. After visiting, listening, and observing, I have walked away from this experience thinking that I now have an "open mind" to the idea that just possibly there is an afterlife where our loved ones are watching us, loving us, and guiding us.

I didn't find the perfect bagel, or that slice of New York quality pizza, but I did find North Carolina barbecue, sweet tea, and a friend I will have for life.

Introduction

Gateway City and Ghost Vortex

> "Ghosts need human energy to thrive.
> There are no living people in a cemetery,
> so why would you think that's where you'd find them?"
> -- *Author's Mother, Joan*

As a researcher, who wouldn't want to write a haunted historical city book about Greensboro, North Carolina? This is one of those cities where so much significant history has occurred, and yet, it's as if no one knows about it. I suppose that's because, besides being an "old soul," there is a quiet dignity that is prevalent throughout the city. It doesn't scream "Look at me, I have tourist attractions, baseball teams, and ghosts!" like other places do. That's because it doesn't have to; it's not completely dependent on tourist dollars nor is it at the mercy of the weather. It's because of that financial independence that it is able to welcome anyone who drops by for a visit, offer any hospitality that is asked for or sought after, and deliver what it promises on the first go round. The city's treasures are not worn on its coat sleeve for any passerby to glean, judge, and then move on, but rather, like all great treasures, it shares its secrets only with those it takes into its confidence.

In doing my research on the Gateway City, a place where I had the pleasure to live for some years, I had no real idea of its history and historical significance until I began exploring it in depth and asking questions for the very book you are reading now. I had not

Gateway City and Ghost Vortex

heard of any of its ghostly apparitions or hauntings—until I asked. It was only then, with a little gentle pulling and prodding, that the information I sought began to creep out from its hiding places, tentatively testing the sunlight it was about to enter into, and, eventually, find its way to me.

To be honest, it was something of a task to collect these stories, after all Greensboro is a fairly large and productive city. Its residents are hardworking and, generally speaking, are serious-minded, spiritual, and not inclined to spread gossip, which, after all, is what I was sort of asking them to do. Basically, a ghost story requires a haunted location, which generally means something tragic or at least horribly sad had to have happened there, thereby creating the very precise circumstances that are necessary to have a haunting occur. Then I come along, asking a lot of nosy questions and looking for the bad news of days gone by, picking at old wounds.

In the defense of those who call the Piedmont Triad area home, I was an unknown on many levels. True, by this time, I had two other books to my writing credit, had been on numerous TV and radio shows, and appeared in scores of newspaper articles, and not just national TV, radio, and print, but in their own local media as well. No, it wasn't that. The wall I kept hitting was not due to my credentials, but rather, to my intent. What was I going to do with the secrets I was seeking? How was I going to represent the people, their history, and their city? A fair concern and one I promised that I would take to heart.

As a researcher and chronicler of information, I would tell potential sources that it is most important to me that the history of the city of Greensboro be properly recorded for its future generations. I'm simply telling the story of various historical and otherwise seemingly mundane locations, be they businesses or private residences, which among other tidbits of curious information, happen to be haunted. That too is part of a place's history that needs to be recorded somewhere. As to whether or not I personally believe in the existence of ghosts or vampires or demons is completely irrelevant for my writing the history, as this book is not about what I believe or what I feel you should believe, but rather, what has time and again been reported. Is it real? Did it happen? Can it be

Introduction

true? How is it possible? I'll present you with all the information that I have gathered and you, the reader, will need to come to your own drawn conclusions.

What I found to be most interesting is that there were no stories that took place specifically in a cemetery. I had naturally assumed that there would be a few ghost stories like that; after all, my last book was a historical reference guide to vampires and lots of different species of vampires from various cultures haunt graveyards and cremation grounds. And there are numerous folktales that take place in cemeteries as well. It just seemed like a natural progression. However, it was my mom, the brilliant woman that she is, who pointed out to me that: "Ghosts need human energy to thrive. There are no living people in a cemetery, so why would you think that's where you'd find them?"

Mother not only knows best, she knows everything. I stand humbly corrected.

There is one last thing that I would like to point out about the various chapters and the information they contain. It is interesting, and a little frightening as well, that so many of the stories and places share a history and cross over with one another. Who would ever guess, for instance, that a local dog-grooming business might be connected to the local and aggressive forerunner of women's suffrage? Or that something so simple and elusive as a soil sample that had been thought to have been destroyed long ago has not only been found because of the research that was necessary for the writing of this book, but that it could provide critical bits of information regarding one of the nation's most haunted places? Keep in mind that so many of these haunted locations are, for the most part, around the same area of town. It could be a coincidence, but maybe there's something to it.

So here it is. I present to you the history of eighteen historic and haunted locations to be found in and around the city of Greensboro, North Carolina, the Gateway City, The Star of the Triad, and the place I have come to consider my friend.

1

Welcome to Greensboro, North Carolina

Piedmont Triad Area

> "There is no excellent beauty that hath not some strangeness in the proportion."
> -- *Sir Francis Bacon (1561–1626)*

The Gateway City

The first settlers to the area began to trickle in during the 1740s. Guilford County was formed in 1771 and the town of Greensborough, as it was originally spelled back then, was founded in 1808. The initial slow-growing town of Greensborough had 369 residents as of 1821. These early settlers owned and operated their own small farms where they typically raised cattle, corn, pork, and wheat. It was a hard provincial life and turning a profit at market was no easy task as there were no nearby large cities driving up prices. This meant that money was, for the most part, washing back and forth amongst the same people.

The land for Greensborough was purchased for $98 and was described as being an "unbroken forest with thick undergrowth of huckleberry bushes that bore a finely flavored fruit." Using the Consumer

Chapter One

The Lincoln Financial tower is the tallest building in downtown Greensboro, and it is the first building visitors will see as they head towards downtown. Depending on the direction they are coming from, they'll see it from miles away.

Welcome to Greensboro, North Carolina

Modern buildings mingle nicely in the downtown skyscape.

Chapter One

The Memorial water fountain releases a cool water squirt to anyone who would care to experience a quick and refreshing spray of water.

Welcome to Greensboro, North Carolina

Wrangler has been located in Greensboro ever since the Cone Brothers opened up Proximity Mills back in 1895.

Price Index Scale, that would be the equivalent of paying about $39,080 today.

Greensborough was a planned city, and it was decided that at its center point would be the location of the courthouse. The idea behind this was that with the courthouse in the geographical center of the county, it would be equidistant and easily reached by all its citizens. The first three streets of the town—Davie, Elm, and Greene—were to run north to south and intersect with its first three east to west streets: Gaston, Market, and Sycamore. At the corners of Market and Elm Streets stood the courthouse.

The developing town was named Greensborough to honor the American Revolutionary War hero Major General Nathanael Greene. On March 15, 1781, he commanded the American Continental troops at the Battle of Guilford Court House against British General Charles E. Cornwallis. (See section "Guilford County Courthouse"; please note: the word *courthouse* was spelled as two separate words back then.)

Chapter One

Surrounded by the skyscrapers of Greensboro, this park has a cozy feel to it.

Welcome to Greensboro, North Carolina

Although the battle was lost, it was through Greene's next series of actions that allowed the Americans to shortly thereafter win the war by giving his fellow Americans and General George Washington critical time to prepare to meet and defeat the enemy at the Battle of Yorktown. At this time the population of Greensborough was a little over 2,100.

The town developed at a slow and steady pace, but in the 1840s, though its population had not even quite doubled, Governor Morehead requested and was granted a new railroad line that caused the town to develop into a village. The railroad proved to be key in the growth of the village, as it soon became the transportation hub for the state, earning for itself the nickname "The Gate City." It followed that with rail transportation made easy, textile mills would move in, and, indeed they did, many of those who did take advantage of the rail system remain here today—Wrangler, Lee, and Galey and Lord, just to name a few.

Because of the cotton trade, wealth finally began to generate in Greensborough, allowing for the construction of a few notable homes such as Blandwood Mansion, 1844 (see "Blandwood Plantation" section); the Bumpass-Troy House, 1847; and Dunleith, 1856.

In the final days of the War Between the States when the Confederate Cabinet members left their capital city of Richmond, Virginia, they decided to reconvene in Greensborough, North Carolina. For five long and stressful days, the city served as the South's new capital. At the same time, Governor Zebulon B. Vance, in anticipation of the invading Union troops, fled North Carolina's state capital. He relocated it and himself both in the city of Greensborough. It was in the parlor room of Blandwood Mansion that Governor Vance surrendered himself and his state to Union troops on April 28, 1865. He has been quoted as saying "Greensborough witnessed not only the demise of the Confederacy but also that of the old civil government of the state [of North Carolina]." (See "Blandwood Plantation" section.)

After the war, during the Reconstruction Period, northern developers such as Caesar and Moses Cone came to Greensborough in 1890 when its population was just over 3,300 people. Here, the Cone brothers developed large-scale textile mills that turned the

Chapter One

village into a city in about ten years. By 1900 the city's population had exploded to over 10,000 residents (see "Biltmore Hotel" and "Salon Blu'" sections).

In 1895 the spelling of *Greensborough* was officially changed to *Greensboro*. Although not a proven fact, popular consensus claims that this was done so that the newly developing city would look less provincial on paper as it now had the reputation for and was considered by many to be the center of the southern textile industry. Again, the boom of industry showed a surge in the construction of prominent buildings such as a new Guilford County Courthouse, West Market Street Methodist Church, and the main building for the University of North Carolina at Greensboro.

A mural portrait of General Green can be found on one of the buildings amidst the hustle and bustle of downtown.

The population continued to grow, the city continued to expand, and the wealth continued to be stockpiled as the twentieth century wore on. Real estate in 1920s Greensboro was called "the wonder of the state." It even prospered during the Depression era and developed a reputation for being a well-developed community with quality education. Greensboro's population had doubled again, and over 20,000 people now enjoyed life in this city with numerous parks and many companies

Welcome to Greensboro, North Carolina

that were always looking to hire on more hands. It was during this booming time that the story of *Lydia, the Phantom Hitchhiker*, was first told (see "Lydia" section).

The 1940s were very prosperous times for the city. With residency now at 600,000 there was more than an ample work force to fill positions. The mill that the Cone brothers had founded was now the world's largest producer of denim and Sears Roebuck and Company had built a regional catalogue distribution center.

In the following decade, Lorillard Tobacco Company built a manufacturing company here, and the Moses Cone Memorial Hospital opened a brand new, state of the art regional medical center. Public housing was being built all over the city, the first Downtown Revitalization Committee was formed, as well as the long-awaited for coliseum that was finally built on the old fair grounds. The 1950s ended with a Memorial being erected and dedicated to the soldiers who bravely fought and gave their lives during World War II and the Korean War.

Another significant historical moment occurred in the city of Greensboro on February 1, 1960, when four black college students sat down at the whites only counter at Woolworth's. Service to them was denied, as this was a time of racial segregation. The brave students refused to leave and, in doing so, started a sit-in that lasted several long months, had hundreds of other local citizens joining in, and eventually led to the desegregation of not only Woolworth's but many other stores as well. The actual lunch counter where this event took place now sits in the Smithsonian Museum in Washington, DC. Over 120,000 people were now living in Greensboro at this historic time.

Sadly, the downtown area of Greensboro did not fare well during this time. Although a parking deck and urban renewal was already underway, Four Seasons Town Center and the Carolina Circle Mall had already opened and lured shoppers to them.

Greensboro's schools were fully integrated in the 1970s and was recognized nationwide for its success. Sadly, later that same decade, five people were killed in a Klan-Nazi and Communist Worker's Party (CWP) confrontation. This incident was captured on film and broadcast nationwide. Six Klan members were arrested and put on trial for the murders, but, due to circumstances that are still muddy to this day, the men were acquitted.

Chapter One

Walking out of the Cultural Center this breathtaking view of one of the parks downtown greets visitors.

Welcome to Greensboro, North Carolina

Four new skyscrapers added their profile to the city's skyline in the 1980s while a new airport terminal was completed, the Piedmont Triad International.

The millennium ended on a scholarly note for the city. A new public library opened up downtown; a children's museum opened next to the city's historical museum; and a budding theater district tried its wings on Elm Street. It was also during this time that it was first suggested that the old Woolworth's building be turned into a Civic Rights Museum.

The city has also been home to many famous Americans, such as Orson Scott Card, a Hugo and Nebula Award-winning author; Joey Cheek, an Olympic gold medal winner; famed short story writer, William Sydney Porter, better known to the public as O. Henry; and Dough Marlette, a Pulitzer Prize-winning cartoonist.

Today, all 109 square miles of the city is framed between I-40, I-71, and I-85. Some 240,000 people call Greensboro home, making it the largest city in Guilford County, the county seat, and the third largest city in the state.

Other little tidbits of information about the city to round out this section—the oak leaf is prominent in the symbolism of Greensboro. Just about everywhere you look, the city's logo is proudly stamped on something. The swooping green "G" ends in a nicely stylized oak leaf. The official flag of the city, not surprisingly, has the emblazoned image of General Nathanael Greene on it, an image of gold on a field of green. It's the image of the general atop his mount, taken from his equestrian statue located in Guildford County Historic Park. On the flag, a wreath of oak surrounds the general. The city's seal has the original spelling of the city on it (Greensborough). Back in 1808, when it was officially incorporated, the town of Greensboro was only a quarter of a mile wide and long. The seal bears the likeness of what I suspect to be the goddess Victory surrounded by an enclosed wreath of oak. The only place the oak does not play a prominent role, and I suspect only because it otherwise cannot, is as the city's official flower. The "Greensboro Red Camellia Japonica" was adopted as the city's official flower on May 3, 1965. It is noteworthy for its ability to withstand extreme cold, drought, and heat. Just like the oak.

Aycock Auditorium

> "The educated differ from the uneducated as much
> as the living from the dead."
> -- *Aristotle (384–322 BC)*

The University of North Carolina at Greensboro (UNCG) was founded February 18, 1891, through a legislative grant. The city of Greensboro was selected because of its location in the virtual geographical center of the state, thereby making it equally accessible to anyone who wished to attend. Women traveled from all over North Carolina to attend school there. This was a considerable undertaking, as this was the Reconstruction Period that took place after the Civil War. Women who were fortunate and could cover the cost took a train into the city. Most of the women who attended the school, however, had to travel by horse and buggy, a long and hazardous undertaking.

UNCG was the first North Carolina state-supported school of higher education specifically for women. The idea at the time was that if women were educated, then they would feel a desire to educate their children, and that would raise the overall level of educated people in the state. Its original name was the State Normal and Industrial School, but it underwent numerous name changes over the years before becoming UNCG. The school was founded largely by the efforts of Charles Duncan McIver, a renowned advocate for women's education. Its original ten-acre plot of land

Aycock Auditorium

was a gift to the school from R. T. Gray and R. S. Pullen. Its first building, paid for by state funds, cost $30,000. Using the Consumer Price Index Scale, that would be the equivalent of paying about $700,000 today.

On October 5, 1892, the school opened its doors for business, and its fifteen faculty members taught to a student body of 223 that first year. Charles McIver had the pleasure of serving as the school's first president. Over the years that position's name changed too. Now the position is called chancellor.

In addition to a statue of his likeness erected in his honor (referred to as "Charlie" by the student body), there is also a building, a parking deck, and a street on campus all of which are named to honor him.

During the college's first years, although prosperous and successful in attracting big-time investors such as Andrew Carnegie, it saw more than its fair share of hardships. There was a typhoid epidemic; a fire that destroyed Brick Dorm and displaced many students; and the sudden passing of Charles McIver, the driving force behind the college.

Chapter Two

In the year 1897, the school changed its name for the first time, from State Normal and Industrial School to State Normal and Industrial College. In 1903, seven students received the first Bachelor's degrees given out by the college.

The school grew and became even more successful. The Women's Suffrage Movement was playing a key part on campus, as many of the faculty and students alike were very active in this noble endeavor.

In 1912 the college invited President Theodore Roosevelt to come and be a guest speaker, which he gladly did to a student body of 700. Robert B. Harris was the first male student to enroll at the college in 1914. In 1919 the college again changed its name, this time to North Carolina College for Women.

During the 1920s the college enjoyed a time of prosperity and several new buildings were added to the campus. However, the 1930s hit the college hard, and because of this sudden economic need, it made allowances for male enrollment as daytime-only students. Due to the merging of the State Normal and Industrial College with the North Carolina College of Agriculture and Engineering, it changed its name to the Women's College of the University of North Carolina. Author Thornton Wilder and scientist George Washington Carver also visited the college during these times.

During the 1940s the college attracted such notable speakers as First Lady Eleanor Roosevelt, on two separate occasions, as it began to slowly recover from the nation's previous Depression. During the 1950s the campus began to change as many of the founders of the college stepped down and new blood stepped in. In 1956 the college, in a very progressive move, was officially integrated. At this time, the city of Greensboro was still racially segregated. If this hurt enrollment, it was hard to tell, as now over 2,500 students were attending the college.

Like many college campuses across the nation, the changes that were happening in the world were being reflected on campus. In 1960 students from the college took part in the now-famous Woolworth's sit-in. In 1963 the school officially went co-ed and changed its name yet again, now to the University of North Carolina

Aycock Auditorium

at Greensboro. Many of its alumni still refer to it as the Women's College, or "the WC."

Throughout the 1970s to today, the college has only continued to grow, both with the quality of teachers and facilities, and students choosing to attend. Today, 12,000 students roam the 180-acre campus, and of the seventy-two buildings on campus, three have had ghostly sightings reported—*but only Aycock Auditorium is reputed by EVERYONE to be haunted*.

In the 1920s, during the college's first true run of prosperity, it purchased a nearby parcel of land on which it built a theater. This property had an old and abandoned house on it, and was known to be the former residence of the late Jane Aycock. It is said that the students were already familiar with the property and the house, as they would dare one another to go inside the abandoned structure and bravely enter into the attic. This was said to be the place where its former owner and sole occupant had committed suicide.

After the purchase of the property, it was never the intent of the college to use the actual house for anything; the school was only interested in the land. The old home was razed to the ground and the rubble cleared away.

The auditorium was in fact named after a North Carolina governor, Charles Brantley Aycock, who sat in office from 1901 to 1905. In a plan to boost the state's economy, he launched a massive educational initiative. Some people will say that the theater was named after his daughter, Jane, but this is not the case. As a matter of historical record, the good governor had no daughter by that name that he ever admitted to or modern day research can connect him with. There is no indication of them being blood related.

Construction of Aycock Auditorium was completed in 1926 and opened for use in 1928.

On campus, the most popular, traditional telling of the tale of the haunting of Aycock Auditorium claims that young Jane hung herself in the old house's attic. She is said to have done so during a fit of depression caused by the sudden and unexpected death of her fiancé. The thought of life without him by her side was simply more than she could bear, making suicide look like a viable option.

Chapter Two

Other students will say that she was a lonely old woman who never married and had no family. They say that near the end of her days she could not bring herself to face death alone and could tolerate her solitary existence no longer. Again, by an undisclosed means of suicide, Jane took her life in her unhappy home's attic. Naturally, there is a combination of the two tales, and my personal favorite as well. This final version claims that Jane, devastated by the death of her beloved, was never able to recover from the loss and wasted her life away. Finally, as an old woman, she succumbed to the ever-mounting sadness and took her life in the attic of the home she had singularly occupied for so many empty years.

No matter which origin of the story you prefer, there is a lonely female ghost to suit your needs. Jane's ghostly form has been described in numerous ways over the years, lending credence to all of the creation myths mentioned above: *as an elderly woman, as a young lady dressed in a long white gown, as a cloudy mass moving of its own accord, as a ball of light, as a shadowy form on a balcony, and as nothing more than a "female" presence in the room.*

Typically Jane, in one of her many incarnations, is most often encountered in the theater's basement. Although she has never harmed anyone or done anything even hinting at being violent, those who have experienced an incident with Jane in the basement often swear that they will never return down there again. Further, they say that if they absolutely must return to the basement, for any length of time, they will not do so alone.

In addition to the basement, Jane is also, allegedly, sighted as a shadowy figure up in the theater's balcony. She has been seen both sitting in one of the many seats as well as standing at the railing. Occasionally there is a report of her moving from one dark place in the balcony to another and then eventually...out of sight. Some folks like to speculate that Jane is seen up in the balcony so often because it is the highest accessible public point in the building, and she has adopted this lofty area as a reasonable replacement for the attic she died in.

Reports of Jane being seen or experienced outside the theater are rare, but one is made each generation. In these cases she is

Aycock Auditorium

described as being just outside the building, not more than a few feet from the walls. It may be that if Jane is not bound specifically to Aycock Auditorium, then perhaps she is also responsible for some of the other ghostlike activity that occurs on campus. We'll never know for sure, but it's a thought to consider.

Although many faculty and students alike claim to have experienced Jane and her poltergeist pranks over the years, she has only ever appeared in her ghostly form to men. Women, for whatever reason, have only ever heard her or been witness after-the-fact to objects that the ghost has allegedly moved.

Events and activities accredited to Jane have been reported as stage lights coming on by themselves, neatly stacked piles of costumes and clothing inexplicably scattered about the room, the piano playing a few sad keys with no one apparent sitting at its bench, doors bursting open with a sudden and abrupt gust of icy air, heavy chains heard rattling off in the distance, cold radiators suddenly hissing when the heat has not been turned on, radios turning themselves on or off, the blare of trumpet music being heard, the sound of footsteps echoing off the empty stage, sewing machines starting up and running full throttle, and perhaps the most frightening of all is the pressure of a hand resting on your shoulder when you are alone.

Aycock Auditorium is located at the corner of Spring and Tate streets. The UNCG Box Office and Information Center sells both individual tickets and season passes. You can purchase either over the phone by calling 336-334-4849 or by visiting their Web site at www.uncg.edu/euc/boxoffice.

3

Biltmore Hotel

> "Life grants nothing to us mortals without hard work."
> *-- Horace (65 BC–8 BC)*

When I was out doing my research for the Carolina Theatre, my assistant, Joy, turned to me and pointed to a building standing behind us. "I bet that place is haunted." She said it quite matter-of-factly, with the same deliberate certainty that a person would also say "I bet water is wet." I turned to see what she was pointing at, fully expecting to gaze upon an old or broken-down building. That very fact alone I must say would have surprised me, as downtown Greensboro is in something of a brilliant and modern revitalization. Instead what I saw was a simple shingle hanging under a domed awning over a set of huge and heavy-looking oak doors with brass fixtures. The sign read "The Biltmore Inn."

Moses Cone is a name well known in the city of Greensboro and it's usually in connection with either his textile empire or the Moses H. Cone Memorial Hospital that was established in 1953 by his widow, Bertha Cone. But most people are unfamiliar with who the man was, why he is important to the city of Greensboro, or what his connection to the Biltmore Hotel is.

Born in 1857 to German immigrants and the oldest of thirteen children, Moses, along with his brother Caesar, went about expanding the family's already existing green grocer business. Many of their clients were the grocers who sold food to the textile mills in North Carolina.

Biltmore Hotel

Chapter Three

It was typical for the Cone brothers to accept bolts of fabric in lieu of cash payment from these businesses. The Reconstruction period was underway in the South at this time and actual paper money was hard for many businesses to come by. Accepting shipments of fabric was better than allowing for credit, as the brothers were then able to sell the fabric for more money than the food shipment was worth to them. Naturally they were increasingly willing to accept textiles as a means of payment from their grocery suppliers who preferred this method of currency. By making this one highly logical and profitable business decision, to trade in fabric, the brothers established the Cone Export and Commission Company. More and more of their business and social connections were coming from the textile industry, so the Cone brothers decided to make it official—they would move to Greensboro, North Carolina, and open a new branch of the Cone Export and Commission Company there.

In 1895 the brothers built a mill for themselves, simply naming it "Proximity" because they had decided to have it built in the midst of the railway, warehouses, and raw cotton suppliers of what is now downtown Greensboro. Buyers from businesses right across the street could walk inside, examine the goods, buy on the spot, and literally walk right back across the street with their purchase to be processed or transported. With no need to charge for shipping, the Cone brothers were able to sell at a better rate than their competitors. It was at this mill where Moses became known as the "Denim King" because it was at Proximity Mill that they were making their trademark "heavy duty, deep tone, blue denim."

The Proximity Manufacturing Company headquarters was a declaration to opulent luxury meeting modern know-how, especially because it was to many local residences and business owners "just a mill after all." Moses Cone spared no expense when he ordered the construction of the Romanesque-style mill headquarters complete with the additional flair of fancy brickwork for his business in 1895. Of particular and startling note to the first onlookers of the completed building was the fact that there were no chimneys or fireplace stacks to be seen. This was because the Cone brothers' new building did not need them, as it was heated and powered completely by electricity.

Biltmore Hotel

Proximity Manufacturing Company went on to expand under the Cone brothers' leadership. Thirty plants provided jobs and financial security to the hardworking people of Greensboro. To this day, the company that the brothers founded still provides denim to Levi Strauss and Company. Moses eventually faded out of the textile business to pursue work in conservation and philanthropy, leaving the day-to-day running of the company to his brother Caesar. Moses died shortly thereafter, in 1908.

In 1911 the building could no longer contain the ever-increasing business that the Cone brothers had created. In need of more space, Caesar sold the building to the city of Greensboro and moved the company to a newer, larger building on Green Street. For nine years what was the Proximity Mill building was now home to the city's first post office.

In 1920 the old Proximity Mill building was again too small for its newest intended purpose. It was sold to a private investor who had plans to turn the old post office into a grand hotel. The investor had wanted to open a luxurious hotel the likes of which the city had never before seen. Aside from the usual amenities that any grand hotel of that day and age would offer, this one would proudly boast of having a private bath in every room with hot and cold running water. So grandiose and unprecedented an idea did not sit well with the City Council. At a charge of $2 a night, they did not see any hotel, no matter how splendid or wonderful, being able to stay open for very long. That was what the average local employee was making in a week. In today's market, that would be the equivalent of taking home a little over $300 dollars for a week's pay. Imagine using your entire paycheck to spend one night in a hotel. The City Council members could not either. It was because of this that it took the investor two years to finally get permission from them to open the Greensboro Inn.

Little did the City Council members know back then that the Greensboro Inn would not only make enough money to keep its doors open, but it would also do very well, even through the Great Depression. Even at $2 a night. In fact, numerous Presidents, kings, and queens have slept there.

In the 1940s the Greensboro Inn was sold. The new owners changed the name to the Greenwich Inn in honor of Lord Greenwich.

Chapter Three

It was in the 1950s that the building currently being called the Greenwich Inn began to feel the effects of a difficult economy for the first time. The downtown area was falling out of favor with the local residents, a fate that the Carolina Theatre was suffering from as well (see "Carolina Theatre" section). The once great hotel that had played host to Presidents and royalty alike was now finding itself reduced to being nothing more than a common flophouse. It was sadly typical to see prostitutes working the corner under the watchful eye of their pimp. Rooms at the Greenwich Inn were being rented by the hour just to make ends meet.

In 1960 a fire broke out on the third floor of the inn, mercifully closing it down. It was perhaps the first lucky break the building had gotten in some time. A group of investors from New York City purchased it shortly thereafter. They got it at a steal, having only to pay the city its back taxes. The investors hired the nationally renowned and local designer Otto Zenke to be the decorator and oversee the project. Zenke was North Carolina's premier designer and a celebrity in his own right, what we would call a "decorator to the stars" today. Zenke had his own distinctive style and was well known to work very fast, earning him the nickname of "Instant Otto." Zenke is probably best known for his work at the White House, hired by then First Lady, Jacqueline Kennedy.

Much of the artwork that hangs in the hotel today was purchased by Zenke from a local gallery that specialized in promoting the work of local artists. Zenke had decided to model the hotel after an English hunting club. All brand-new, carved, and heavy wood furniture was purchased for the timeless look. The lobby was covered in rare wood flooring and paneling that went up to the ceiling. Brass fixtures abounded. To look at it, one would never know that a hundred years before it was the Cone brothers' Proximity Mill spinning out bolt after bolt of deep-blue-colored denim.

In 1970 the New York City investors sold it, and the new owners renamed it the Biltmore. Despite local and popular misconception, they did not name it after the estate of the same name that stands in Asheville, North Carolina, but rather for a far more pragmatic purpose. At that time the name *Biltmore* was rather popular, as hundreds of hotels and inns sharing that very same name nationwide would attest. The

Biltmore Hotel

new owners felt that the name sounded dignified, familiar, prestigious, and the very image of luxury. That's why they chose it.

Sadly, this newest set of owners were not as on top of things as they could have been. The live-in managers that were hired to run and maintain the business let little repairs slide and turned a blind eye when they began to need more attention. It was beginning to look like the Biltmore was once again facing another slow and painful deterioration.

Then, a few years ago, led by developer Milton Kern, six Greensboro businessmen came together to form Bogart's Hall Investment Co. They purchased the Biltmore in October of 2007 for a little less than $2 million dollars. Thanks to these men, this historic hotel is not just in the hands of local ownership again, but rather the building itself—and its history—have been saved. These newest owners have decided to keep the hotel open while they perform a series of slow but constant upgrades and restorations.

The Biltmore Hotel is three stories tall, boasting twenty-six guest rooms and is absolutely beautiful, inside and out. Each room, with its fourteen-foot-tall ceilings and historically accurate paint and color schemes, has more than the typical hotel amenities, such as a coffee maker, iron, and cable TV. For instance, each piece of furniture throughout the hotel is a genuine antique, masterfully restored, and was originally purchased by Otto Zenke himself some forty years ago. Every room has a gorgeous antique bed covered with brand-new pillows and linens. Everything else in the room, including the throw rugs and curtains, are hand-selected for each individual room's flair and style from the local Macy's department store.

The Biltmore Hotel also has a large conference center, workout room, and free wifi connections. From six to seven every evening there is a complimentary wine tasting in the lobby open to guests of the hotel and sponsored by Stonefield Winery of Stokesdale, North Carolina.

When you first open the tall and thick wooden doors to the lobby of the Biltmore, it will blow you away. Suddenly you are transported back in time from a modern city street to the very heart of an English-inspired study. The walls are covered with the same wood paneling Zenke installed and the shelves are filled with books. An intricately carved wooden deer head hangs over a faux fireplace and the floor, brightly

Chapter Three

This Thomas Gainesborough's painting of Lord Greenwich is easily ten feet tall and dominates the lobby it hangs in. It is one of the many fine pieces of artwork that hangs throughout the Biltmore Hotel. Lord Greenwich was said at one time to have been a governor of North Carolina.

polished and beautiful, gently creaks cricket-like beneath your feet. A modest check-in counter is there, of course, but it's unobtrusive and blends into its surroundings well. What dominates the room and commands your respect and attention, however, is a large portrait of Lord Greenwich, painted by the artist Thomas Gainesborough. "Boy in Blue" is perhaps Gainesborough's most recognizable painting, that of a youngish lord handsomely dressed in a silken blue suit and standing in a wispy brown landscape. Nevertheless, Lord Greenwich in all his glory is a sight to behold.

Mr. Ronnie Dennison has been employed at the Biltmore Hotel for some years now, working his way up from a third-shift desk clerk to the general manager position he holds today. Dennison knows the entire history of the hotel, going all the way back to the Cone brothers—*and he also knows the history of the two resident ghosts that haunt the Biltmore.*

Dennison told me that in life, she was a small, frail, and petite woman. Her long black hair was worn loose and down past her shoulders, and that when she walked, she did so quickly, heels clicking against the floor loudly. She frequented the outside steps to the side

Biltmore Hotel

Taken from the top of the two-story-tall stairwell, this is the very flight of stairs that "Wendy" was thrown down, shattering her body, no doubt killing her long before she reached the pavement below. At the time of her death, these stairs were not enclosed as they are today, but rather, were on the outside of the hotel. They led directly to the second floor, allowing patrons the option of discretion if they needed it.

Chapter Three

of the hotel that led directly to the second story. That was where she, like many "professional women" back in the 1960s, kept a room. One night she and her pimp got into one last and fatal fight. In a fit of rage, the pimp violently shoved the little woman down the straight flight of stairs, two full stories, to the pavement below.

Her real name sadly has been lost, but she will not let herself be forgotten. One of the staff started calling her "Wendy" when the ghost began to make her presence known. The name has stuck. Every once in a while you can hear a lithe and quick-stepping person racing up the stairs, high heels clicking and echoing in the stairwell that had been enclosed by Zenke in his revamp of the building.

The Biltmore was the first hotel in the city to install a full-service Warner Brand elevator, and it's still in perfect operating condition. It's a bit on the small side but wood lined, and when the buttons are pushed, the magnet-driven machine leaps into action, taking you to your desired destination. It was a pretty amazing piece of technological advancement when it was installed, and Wendy seems to enjoy riding it. Many staff and guests of the hotel have reported seeing through the elevator's circular window a woman fitting Wendy's description. They know it's Wendy because when the elevator stops and you open the door and brass gate, the small cart is shockingly empty.

The room that she rented out in life is one of the seventeen rooms that now, having been newly renovated, feature a king-size bed. I've not included the exact room number by request of the management, but if you go and stay there, perhaps you can convince one of the staff to tip you off. Her room is now brilliantly decorated and accented, and Wendy must be very fond of it. General Manager Dennison told me that if you place your hand on her door and listen at it, sometimes you can not only hear the rush of wind and the sound of things inside moving about, you can feel the door vibrating. Admittedly, my assistant Joy and I tried it when we were there, but sadly, Wendy was not in.

Many of the guests of the hotel have reported seeing Wendy. Usually they tend to see her walking ahead of a group of people in the narrow hotel hallways. She has never bothered anyone and is, in all reports, completely harmless. Wendy just seems to enjoy her newfound existence

Biltmore Hotel

Here is a view of one of the seventeen guest rooms that have a king-size bed. Although this particular room is not Wendy's, you can see why she would enjoy spending her afterlife in such a place.

at the Biltmore, walking the halls like she owns the place, riding up and down in the elevator, and racing quickly up and down the flight of stairs that caused her early demise.

The other resident ghost who lingers on at the Biltmore Hotel is not nearly as well liked as Wendy, nor is he having a pleasant afterlife either. In fact, he's an altogether rather sad and desperate sort of character.

A psychic who once visited the hotel a couple of years ago named him "Philip," and she has been the only person who has been able to tell us anything about him. She claims that he worked for the Cone

Chapter Three

"Philip" is the other ghost that inhabits the Biltmore. He was once an employee of Ceaser and Moses Cone back when the brothers still ran Proximity Mill. One psychic is credited with telling us that Philip was murdered on the third floor of the mill when he returned one night to retrieve a box he had forgotten to take with him at the end of the day. Garroted from behind, Philip's spirit is now at unrest and is still at the hotel, looking for the box that cost him his life.

brothers back in the days when the building was a mill and the third floor was one wide-open space. Philip went on to explain through her that his famous sibling bosses occasionally had dealings with criminal organizations. He claims, through the psychic, that it was a member of one such association who came up from behind and garroted him

Biltmore Hotel

to death with what he now suspects to have been piano wire. Philip explained to the psychic before contact was lost that he is still at the hotel because he is "looking for the stuff I left here" in a wooden box on the floor.

Unfortunately for Philip, whatever it was that he admitted to having left at Proximity Mill and had need to return to fetch on the night of his murder was most likely taken by the man, or men, who killed him. Nothing of interest has ever been found in the walls or floorboards during any of the hotel's numerous renovations. At least, nothing that has ever been reported. Since no one seems to know what it was that Philip was looking for, what it was that was in the wooden box, there is no way to return it or to help him pass on to the next world since that is what seems to be anchoring him to the hotel.

As a point of interest, I am told that the carpeting in the area where the police found his body back in 1901 has a nasty habit of bubbling up. No matter how many times maintenance is called to go and fix the problem, the carpet always comes undone and bubbles back up. I have to admit that when I was shown the spot, it did appear not to be firmly fastened to the floor. It's believed that the carpet is occasionally pulled up by Philip, determined that he is to find his wooden box where he left it. Dennison told me that this area of the hotel was scheduled for new carpeting soon and hopefully, by the time this book was published, the problem of the carpeting becoming undone would have resolved itself.

Another interesting fact is that one of the part-time employees, a student at one of the local colleges, found an old picture of Proximity Mill that was taken at the turn of the century. As was the custom of the day, all of its employees were lined up and stood outside of their place of employment for the picture. All the people in the photo are named along the bottom of the photograph, and, from what I was told, one of the employees was in fact named Philip.

Again, at the request of the management, I am omitting the room number that Philip is said to most often frequent. Dennison said that he has never had a run-in with this ghost. Philip has historically only appeared to women. There have been many mornings when the desk clerk has heard a lone woman traveler complain about waking up, believing that she saw a man standing at the foot of her bed. But upon

Chapter Three

turning on the bedside lamp, she discovered that she was alone in the room, a relieving, albeit frightening, experience. Other women who have stayed in the room and have not seen Philip manifest have later complained to staff that they had a fitful night, unable to stay asleep or get comfortable. The staff members try not to rent that room out to a single female traveler if they can at all help it.

Attributed to neither Wendy nor Philip specifically, there is also a pretty scary event that happens to whomever is working the front desk on third shift. Dennison remembers it happening to him several times. The windows to the front of the hotel are frosted to about halfway up, letting you see a blurry non-gender specific silhouette of anyone who is moving past the window but nothing clearly until they pass the front doors. On occasion, you can hear the footfalls of a person walking and see their silhouettes moving by, but then *nothing* as they reach the front doors.

Also, the main floor of the hotel is all hardwood and anyone walking on it, even carefully, will make noise. This is especially true of ladies in their high heels. Numerous third-shift desk clerks have said that they can hear the elevator doors open and footfalls coming down the hall, but when the person should appear from around the corner, there is *no one* to be seen. If I had to venture a guess, I'd say that, based on the history of the two ghosts, it's most likely Wendy.

It was the last thing that General Manager Dennison told me as we were leaving the hotel that I personally found to be the most interesting. There have been many occasions where ordinary, everyday people from all walks of life just come into the lobby of the hotel, look at whoever is behind the front desk, and say either "Do you know this place is haunted?" or "The ghosts want me to tell you they're here."

†††††††††††††††

The smoke-free Biltmore Hotel is located in downtown Greensboro at 111 West Washington Street. Despite its history and many amenities, its rates are very competitive at $90 for a standard room, $101 for a Queen, $109 for a King, $120 for a Double, and just $130 for a suite. It is within easy walking distance of many restaurants and shops. For information or to make a reservation, call their toll-free number, 1-800-332-0303, or visit them on the Web at www.thebiltmoregreensboro.com.

†††††††††††††††

4

Blandwood Plantation

> "He who doesn't fear death dies only once."
> -- *Giovanni Falcone (1939–1992)*

It's hard to believe it, but this grand mansion was originally a four-room, two-story, Federal-style farmhouse home. It was constructed in 1795, thirteen years before the founding of Greensborough, and was named Blandwood to honor its builder, Charles Bland.

In 1822 Henry Humphries, a textile industrialist, purchased the property for $50 dollars. Using the Consumer Price Index Scale,

Chapter Four

This wing of Blandwood is called the "Lion Doors" because, as this photo attempts to show, to either side of the front archway is a statue of a lion. It is typical of Italian-style homes to have such decoration on them.

Blandwood Plantation

that would be the equivalent of paying about $860,000 today. Humphries then expanded the house for the first time by adding two more rooms, one on the lower level and one directly above it on the upper level.

Whig Governor John Motley Morehead, known as "the Father of Modern North Carolina," moved into the house in 1826. Blandwood was being used as a rental property by Humphries at that time. Morehead purchased the home for himself in 1827 and lived there on and off until his death in 1866. Although he did not die in the home, he is buried in Greensboro. In fact, there is no record of any births or deaths occurring in the house during Morehead's occupation.

The nationally renowned architect Alexander Jackson Davis was hired in 1844 by Governor Morehead to make his home

FARMHOUSE

Chapter Four

into something really special, an antebellum plantation mansion. Davis designed the country's first Tuscan Villa, Italianate-style home, complete with casement windows, a centralized tower, low rooflines, overhanging eaves, stucco walls, and symmetrical flanking dependencies, which almost doubled the home's square footage.

In 1900 the Keeley Institute purchased the home, and Blandwood was used as an alcoholic rehabilitation clinic and hospital until it closed in 1961.

From 1961 to 1965 the house sat vacant and derelict, falling in disrepair. Fortunately Blandwood did not stay that way for long. It was preserved and saved from demolition when the Greensboro Preservation Society, Inc., purchased it in 1966, deciding to turn it into a museum. An aggressive ten-year restoration process saw to it that Blandwood Mansion was ready to re-open and greet the awaiting public.

Today the fully restored historic house sits atop a hill in the heart of downtown Greensboro. It is the oldest standing example of Italianate architecture in the United States. Additionally, Blandwood also still sits on its original foundation. Surprisingly, many of its original furnishings also remain.

Blandwood Plantation is oozing with rich history. It has housed and played host to many historical characters, intellectuals, and politicians, especially during the Civil War era. Those who had the distinction of having slept there included Confederate General P. G. T. Beauregard; Union Generals Jacob Dolson Cox and John Schofield; Dorothea Dix; and North Carolina State Governor Zebulon B. Vance. It was also the capitol house of both the Confederacy and the state of North Carolina simultaneously, albeit only for a short five-day period. It was the first home in the country to boast Italianate-style architecture and stands even now as the premier and stellar example of the style. Because of all this, Blandwood has been granted the honor of being named a National Historic Landmark, putting it on par and making it peers with the White House.

Blandwood is currently owned by the John Motley Morehead Commission and is operated by the nonprofit organization Preservation Greensboro Incorporated. All that is left of its vast original grounds are

Blandwood Plantation

The Carriage House, as it now stands, fully restored at Blandwood Plantation. No longer used to house buggies, this two-story building now serves as a special events center.

four acres of property that hosts the home's octagonal-shaped carriage house. The carriage house was restored in 1970 and is used now as a special events center.

Ashlee Crayton Poteat is the current manager of the property and was gracious to invite my assistant and me on a private tour. After filling us in on the history of the old mansion, she then told us about the ghost.

He doesn't have a name, but for the sake of storytelling, I will call him "Jack." No one is even sure what time period he may be from. What is certain about him is that he is an afternoon nervous walker, pacing the upstairs hallway.

Poteat suspects, and many of the plantation's staff tend to agree, that Jack must be from when the Keeley Institute owned the property. It is a historical fact that no one was ever born in the mansion, and no one is recorded as having died there either. It is likely that when the property was a plantation, slaves most certainly

Chapter Four

This is the upstairs hallway that resident ghost "Jack" is said to haunt. Most likely a substance-abuse victim in life, he now spends his afternoons pacing the halls. If you're alone in the house around 3 o'clock in the afternoon, you'll most likely hear his heavy footfalls on the hard, wooden floors.

Blandwood Plantation

would have been born and died there, but not in the house itself. Since these connections cannot be made to Blandwood when it was a private residence and certainly not after it became a National Historic Landmark, it stands to reason that whatever unfortunate event occurred to create a ghost would have had to have happened during Keeley's watch.

Many recovering drug and alcohol abusers have a habit of pacing, a trait our ghost is known for. Jack is particularly active in the upstairs hallway around 3 o'clock in the afternoon, a time when the Keeley Institute is said to have begun handing out its evening medications. Perhaps Jack is pacing in anticipation of receiving his medicine, using one drug to overcome another.

Usually only women report hearing Jack, and only when they are alone. But witnesses will swear that Jack sounds like a man walking heel to toe down the hall, and so realistic is the noise he makes them mistakenly believe that a flesh-and-blood someone is in the house with them.

†††††††††††††

Blandwood is located at 447 West Washington Street. It's open to the public Tuesdays through Saturdays 11 a.m. to 2 p.m. and Sundays from 2 to 5 p.m. (Please note that the mansion is closed in January.) Tours are $4 for adults and $2 for children. Group rates are available, but please call ahead to make a reservation. For more information, visit the Web site www.blandwood.org or call 336-272-5003.

†††††††††††††

5

Carolina Theatre

> "One need not be a chamber to be haunted;
> One need not be a house; The brain has
> corridors surpassing Material place."
> *Emily Dickinson (1830–1886)*

If ever you should find yourself in downtown Greensboro and you decide to visit the Carolina Theatre, I cannot express enough that you absolutely must take a tour of the building. It is beautifully restored and as breathtakingly beautiful now as it ever was. Furthermore, if you do visit and opt for the tour, I can only hope that you will be lucky enough to have tour guide extraordinaire Jeffrey "JP" Swisher. There is a story for every brick in the building, and JP knows them all.

Abe and Julian Saenger were two brothers from Shreveport, Louisiana, who one day decided to get out of the drugstore business that they ran and enter into the world of entertainment. They had liked the way E. V. Richards was operating the local theater and invited him in on their business. The three of them soon after incorporated and became Saenger Theaters, Inc. Their first theater, the Saenger, was strictly a vaudeville house, but after one year of operation they decided to dedicate their company to the movie industry.

Richards, although he always stayed involved with the company he helped found with the Saenger brothers, decided to branch out on his own. He became one of history's top men in the motion picture industry. He helped create First National Pictures, Incorporated; he was

Carolina Theatre

Chapter Five

the executive vice president of Public Theaters; and he also worked as a director for Paramount Pictures, Inc. In addition, he owned twenty movie theaters of his own in his home state of Louisiana.

As the years passed by, the Saengers' company began to grow, taking on stockholders. The brothers were only holding fifty percent of the stocks by 1917.

In 1924 the company exploded into business. Theaters were being purchased and built all over the American South, Cuba, Jamaica, Panama, and Puerto Rico. The company had over three hundred theaters in its holdings. It was perhaps not an official trademark of the Saengers' to build very expensive, lavishly opulent, and highly profitable theaters that were then often considered "the pride of" whatever city they were located in; but maybe they just didn't know how to do it any other way. In fact, their theaters were often so well constructed that unless one was willfully torn down to make way for something else, it is still standing today and most likely on a national register of historic buildings.

It was during this sudden boom of business that the Carolina Theatre was commissioned by none other than Julian D. Saenger himself. He had intended for it to act as the company's regional headquarters and wanted it to be a showpiece befitting his intent.

Rather than use his usual architect, Emile Weil, Saenger chose James M. Workman. To build the Carolina according to Saenger's vision, a vaudeville theater and motion picture house, it would cost him no less than $500,000. In 1927, the Carolina became the most expensive theater of its type at that time. Allowing for today's prices, the Consumer Cost Index estimates it would cost over $72 million dollars to reproduce in materials and labor today. Workman had designed other theaters in the past, but he decided to fashion this one into a vaudeville and movie palace extraordinaire, making it into what would become one of the city's most beloved treasures (by building into it a means that would enable it to remain diverse and adaptable). Had Workman not done this, there is little doubt that the Carolina would not be here with us today.

October 31, 1927, was opening day for the Carolina. Greensboro's Mayor Lindley was the first person to purchase a ticket from the Carolina's box office, a right he bragged on proudly. He stood outside

Carolina Theatre

The chandelier that caused a bit of a to-do on opening day, October 31, 1927. It had only just arrived at the theater that morning and needed still to be hoisted into place as 2,000-plus ticket holders stirred restlessly outside, cold and awaiting entry.

Chapter Five

the theater with its Greek temple façade on opening night with over 2,000 other ticket holders. Patiently they waited for the doors to swing wide and give them entrance, but unbeknownst to them, construction was still underway within. The chandelier, which had only just arrived, was being hoisted into place in the grand auditorium's oval-shaped dome. The mayor began to pound with all his might on the doors of the theater demanding entrance, brazenly waving his ticket in his hand. After several long minutes, he and everyone else were welcomed inside and rewarded for their diligence by being the first to see the new and shining chandelier in place.

Back then, the Carolina was lovingly referred to as the "Poor-man's Palace." It had overly tall ceilings, marble floors, evenly placed dark green Corinthian columns with gold-painted capitals, and cornice work throughout. The ceiling was painted in shades of pink and blue to make it resemble a twilight sky. It even had what was called a "powder room" for the ladies and a "Smoking Lounge" for the men. A mural was commissioned for the proscenium arch by famed mural artist Herman Herschauer. It depicted rows of dancing girls. The theater could seat

A breathtaking view of the main lobby, the first spectacle that theatergoers see upon entering through the grand lobby doors.

Carolina Theatre

1,300 ticket holders on thickly cushioned seats on the floor, and another nine hundred in the upper balconies.

For a mere nickel anyone could walk through its doors and feel like a king. Even the "Colored's entrance," with its sandstone floor covered in brightly colored marble tiles, was attractive, if not compared to the front.

There are a bunch of delicious little factoids about this wonderful theater that was new back when Calvin Coolidge was President. For instance, the Carolina was the first commercial, publicly air-conditioned building in the state. It could seat 2,200 people back then. The first musical it showed was "Largo." When the movie "The Jazz Singer" came out, "the first talkie," the Carolina had four showings a day, selling out every seat for every show for two weeks straight in December 1927. If you do the math, that means that over 123,000 folks heard that famous opening line of "Wait a minute, wait a minute, you ain't heard nothin' yet!" over the course of fifty-six different showings.

The two Greek ornamental statues that flank either side of the stage were supposed to be fountains, according to the original design plans. However, if they were to be drinking fountains or the bubbling sort that added atmosphere, no one knows for sure. There is an impression in the floorboards of the stage, the largest built at that time, that supposedly came from the stomping foot of an irate elephant that did not feel like going on stage to perform. The original chandelier and cornice work is still there, and, in the words of James Workman himself, the theater was as "fireproof as modern technology would allow." Quite the haunting bit of foreshadowing.

The Theater had a "Blacks Only" entrance as well as segregated seating in the balcony when it first opened, but sometime in 1964 segregation at the theater began to dissolve of its own accord. By 1965, the Colored Entrance was no longer used and the "Black Balcony," as it was called in its day, was open to anyone who wanted to use it. No city ordinance was passed in order to compel integration and no theater management decree enforced it, it just happened of its own accord, gradually and civilly.

It was also during this time that the city of Greensboro was growing again. Folks were moving out to the suburbs of the city, and in all that wide-open space is where the shopping malls and movie centers

Chapter Five

The stairs that ascend to the upper level and the much acclaimed "Black Balcony." They, along with the columns and carpeting, were damaged in the fire that occurred in the 1980s. They, and the entire lobby itself for that matter, have been restored to how it looked back in the 1920s.

Carolina Theatre

This is one of two statues that stands in the niches to either side of the stage. The original blueprints called for the niches to have fountains. Not only was this vision never fulfilled, but no one is sure if the "fountains" in question were meant to be of the drinking or bubbling variety. The statues, now in place for eighty-two years, were intended to be temporary filler.

Chapter Five

The stage of the Carolina Theater has been the secret to the Theater's long term success. When originally constructed it was intended for both vaudeville performances and the newest means of entertainment—motion pictures.

were being built. People weren't heading into downtown just to see a movie anymore, and hard times began to hit the once much beloved theater.

But unlike other theaters of its time, the Carolina was designed to be adaptable. Its architects and designers may not have known it when they conceived the building at the drawing board, but it is in no small part because of them that we have the theater today. While other theaters fell to the wrecking ball or were forced to show adult movies to make ends meet, there was hope for this once proud and opulent theater yet.

Fortunately, thanks to the United Arts Council and its driving force, Betty Cone, the Carolina Theatre was saved. The UAC raised the money through fund-raising events and the city of Greensboro itself.

There have been numerous renovations done on the Carolina, and seemingly, each time one occurs, she loses more seating. But there was one round of renovations and repairs that happened under a most unfortunate set of circumstances. The downtown residents of Greensboro woke up July 1, 1981, to plumes of jet-black smoke filling the sky. A fire had broken out in their beloved theater. Firefighters rushed to the

Carolina Theatre

scene and began the dangerous task of putting it out. They tried to cut a hole in the four-story building's roof to release some of the smoke but were unable to. The new roof was several inches of solid concrete and more than a match for the chainsaws they tried using.

Luckily the fire was put out and the fifty-four-year-old building dodged another proverbial bullet. The "Black Balcony" had been completely gutted, the lobby severely burned, and extensive smoke damage existed throughout. What was saddest perhaps was the ghastly discovery of a woman's body. She was burned beyond recognition and it took a while to determine her identity.

It has been said that Ms. Melba Frey was a disturbed woman and in need of help. She had limited means and was running low on her psychiatric medicines. She sought out the help of various mental health agencies, but to no avail. It has been said that she was heard leaving one office screaming, "If I don't get my meds, this city is going to burn!"

Frey had tried to make good on her promise. No one is sure how she got into the building, but the story goes that she drank excessively, removed most of her clothing, folded them neatly, and placed them over one of the seats in the "Black Balcony." Perhaps with malicious intent or by innocent accident a fire started. However it happened, Melba Frey died a ghastly and horrific death in the Carolina Theatre.

Reports from witnesses who would rather I not use their names said that her body was eventually discovered in the stairway heading to the balcony and not in the balcony itself. Maybe she was trying to leave. What is certain is that the heat from the flames had reduced her body into a semi-solid gelatinous soup; firefighters did not even recognize it for what it was until after they had walked through it—twice.

Setting the tragedy aside, Carolina Theatre was restored and renovated and opened again for business, this time as the newest member added to the National Register of Historic Places in 1982.

Employees reported a few unusual things that had happened, as in hearing doors open or close. Feeling cold spots, seeing a seat fold up or down. All very creepy in their own right and all can be rationally explained away one way or another, but what is not so easy to dismiss is the ghostly encounter reported by former long-time employee, James Fullbright.

Fullbright was one of the full-time employees working at the theater in the summer of 1989. It was right before another renovation was

Chapter Five

about to occur and the theater was running on a skeleton staff. He and the box office manager at the time, Brian Gray, were the only ones left in the building that day. Fullbright told me that around 4 p.m. Gray was getting ready to leave for the day, and Fullbright said he was right behind him but had a few more things to do before he could feel comfortable leaving as well.

An hour and a half of hard work later, Fullbright was finally getting ready to leave for the day. He left through the back exit, a crash door that would automatically lock behind him. As he was walking out the door, on a whim, he said "Good night" aloud, and just before the crash door closed behind him, he heard a reply, "Good night, James."

For a moment he allowed himself to believe that it was his boss, Gray, who had meant to leave right after saying good-bye earlier but rather lingered as he had. It was very easy to get caught up in one of the many last-minute projects that needed to get done before the next wave of renovations could begin. But then, an instant later he saw that his friend's car was not parked in its usual spot. Fullbright, unable to enter back into the theater because of the automatic locking crash door, ran around to the front of the building. He got in his own car and raced

A view of the stage from the uppermost balcony.

Carolina Theatre

This little bit is about all that remains of the fire damage that was caused back in the 1980s when a distraught Greensboro resident sought to punish the city.

Chapter Five

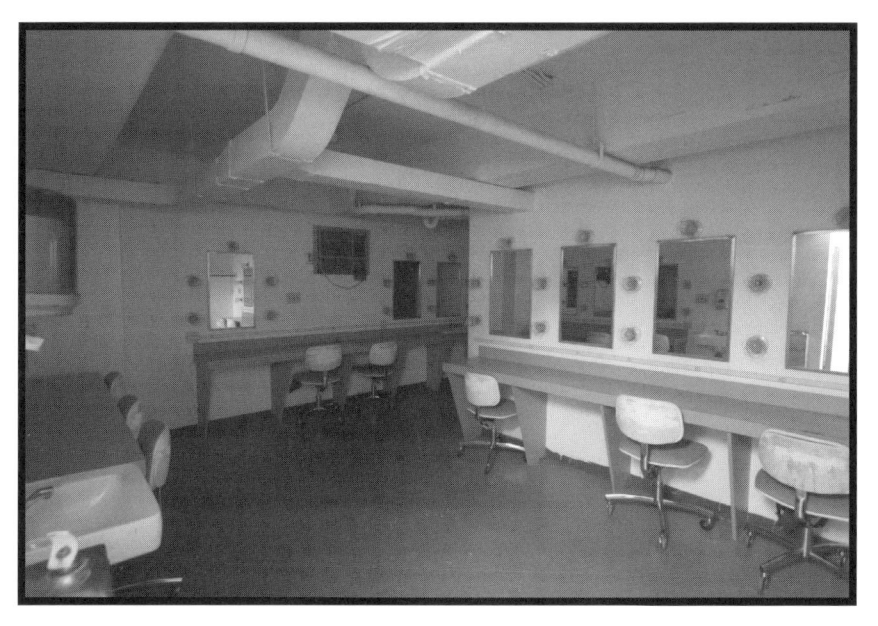

A behind the scenes look at the Carolina. This is the dressing room that hundreds of actors, musicians, and performers have used throughout the years.

home to call his boss, as this was back before the days of cell phones. Gray, who had been home for nearly two hours, answered the phone.

From what I have been told, after that last renovation, the one that restored the "Black Balcony" back to where it could be enjoyed by everyone again, there has been almost no ghostly activity in the Carolina Theatre. It's not too surprising. If the voice that bid James good night was that of Ms. Melba Frey, it would stand to reason that her spirit was bound to the damaged area of the balcony. With that area completely redone with all new materials, there would be nothing left for her to cling to.

†††††††††††††††

Located at 310 South Green Street, Carolina Theatre is open year-round. It shows classic movies, stage productions, and musical concerts. For a full list of scheduled events, please visit the Web site www.carolinatheatre.com or call the box office at 336-333-2605.

†††††††††††††††

6

Private Residence, 419 Cedar Street

> "At first cock-crow the ghosts must go
> Back to their quiet graves below."
> -- *Theodosia Garrison (1874–1944)*

Out behind the new baseball stadium is an area of Greensboro referred to as "the donut." This is because the area all around it has been developed; new housing has been constructed, and it is teeming with the hustle and bustle of traffic and activity. But on Cedar Street, it's a quiet and residential feeling. Cars hardly ever use the road because it doesn't easily cut across or over to any place that a different route doesn't do better. The houses are mostly rented out to folks who leave early in the morning to go to work and begin to come back home between four and six in the evening. It's hard to believe that just a block away is the downtown area filled with buses, commuters, and a constant stream of people.

Richard Welborn told me that he purchased this little green house that was built back in the 1920s in 1993. He says he has no plans of moving anytime soon if he can help it. He likes the area, knows all his neighbors by name, and...*he's OK with the fact that there is a small conclave of ghosts that frequent his living room*.

Welborn owns and operates Pets-U-Love Dog Grooming at 933 South Chapman Street in Greensboro. The business has been open

Chapter Six

since 1982 and caters to all breeds of dogs. Aside from top-notch dog grooming, he also offers canine portraits, obedience training, animal rescue, and astrological readings for both you and your furry friend.

Before he lived here however, Welborn lived in the Arlen House that he said was located on the corner of Friendly and Spring Streets. Sadly, it burned down a number of years ago. He went on to tell me that the Arlen house had been built back in 1897 by the O'Dell family who made their fortune by operating the first hardware store in Greensboro. They were also supporters of the Greensboro Women's College back in the 1920s.

Welborn said that the Arlen House was used by the O'Dell family primarily as more of a private party place. He said that the third floor of the home had at one time been converted into a community movie theater.

Long after the O'Dell's makeshift theater had been closed, the house was turned into a rental property and Welborn said he lived up on the third floor. The door to his room had an oval window in it, and he said that he saw Miss Love Arlen through it, wearing her wedding dress. Love was the sixth child born of the O'Dell family and it was said that she truly loved that house. She had married at 22 and moved with her

Cedar Street

husband to Richmond, Virginia. Missing her family, she came back for a visit not long after her marriage and relocation. It's said that when she finally left to return to her husband, she said good-bye to everyone in such a way that it concerned them deeply that they would never see her again. Unfortunately, this turned out to be true, as she died two weeks later of pneumonia.

The house that Welborn lives in now he says was purchased from the Arlen family. At one time during the 1940s the property was used as a law office, and he recalls one of his neighbors telling him that the head of the law firm was a woman. The name of the woman or the law office he did not recall. He says that from time to time he can hear the voices of many people, never fewer than three, talking about going somewhere, like they are planning a trip, but he can never quite make out where they want to go or to what end.

On an interesting side note, Ms. Louise Brevard Alexander became Greensboro's first female lawyer in 1920 and later went on to become a Juvenile Court Judge. She was key in the campaign for women's suffrage, organizing parades and public protests, and giving speeches. She is perhaps best known in this circle for her enthusiastic call to arms to her female followers to "Raise fewer dahlias and a lot more hell. The place is here. The time is now. The opportunity is yours. It is not the time for women to be alone. They must work together." She taught at the University of North Carolina at Greensboro, what was then called the *State Normal and Industrial College in Greensboro*. She was also the first person ever to receive the O. Max Garner Award in 1949, which is given to distinguished teachers.

Although it is possible and highly probable that Ms. Alexander had a law office in Greensboro, I could not find any such address in my research. I hope to one day be able to devote more time to the matter, because if this humble home of Mr. Welborn's is in fact the first law office of the first female lawyer in Greensboro's history, it would be quite a historical find.

††††††††††††††

Richard Welborn's business, Pets-U-Love dog grooming, is located at 933 South Chapmen Street in Greensboro. Visit www.petsulove.net or call 336-379-7377.

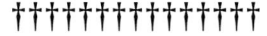

††††††††††††††

7

Rental Property, Chestnut Street

> "Mid pleasures and palaces though we may roam,
> Be it ever so humble, there's no place like home."
> -- *John Howard Payne (1791–1852)*

Former Greensboro resident Stephanie Fischetti told me of a haunted location—an apartment she had lived in for a year on Chestnut Street, a little tan and brown place near the corner of East Hendrix.

She told me that the ghost in her apartment was a good Christian man by reputation, and because of it, she did not want to use his actual name. He enjoyed listening to music, doing carpentry, and having a drink on occasion. Unfortunately, one night the young man had a bit too much to drink and wandered down to the railroad tracks that were behind the rental property. There, he staggered into a parked train, accidentally struck his head against it, and died.

Ms. Fischetti moved into the apartment some five years after the incident. She told me that she experienced a foul smell in the apartment, akin to that of decomposing flesh. Her record player would also turn itself on, and she told me of one time she had returned home from a trip to find that her record player was playing Paul Simon's "Still Crazy After All These Years." But what she found

Chestnut Street

most odd were the four small holes that had been drilled into her wooden storage cabinet. Shavings were still present. Nothing had been moved or stolen in the apartment.

Sharing the apartment with the ghost was not at all a pleasant experience for Ms. Fischetti. She felt a presence in her home she didn't like or want and began to seek a means by which she could be rid of the music-loving specter. Several attempts were made through various channels, but to no success.

Then her luck turned. Just as it was looking like she was going to have to ask a priest to perform an exorcism in her home, one of her neighbors dropped by with a most unexpected guest. She was

Chapter Seven

introduced to a young widow who had lived in the same apartment a few years previous. The widow was curious if she could look at the apartment since there had been some renovation to it from the time when she had lived there with her late husband. Welcomed inside, the guest looked around and noticed that Ms. Fischetti and another friend were in the middle of a tarot card session. The widow, who was a young woman herself, pointed at the cards and asked if they were doing that because of her husband who had died out back.

The two women exchanged stories and it was decided that the music-loving carpenter who had died so tragically young was indeed the ghost haunting the apartment. It was a bittersweet discovery for everyone involved.

The widow went to the area of the house that had been her husband's favorite, and there she prayed for his soul. She asked him to move on from this world and to go to his reward with Jesus.

Ms. Fischetti never experienced another event in her home after that visit. She believes that this ghost was especially lucky. It is her opinion that ghosts that come to be because of a tragic death can linger in a place until a loved one sends them on their way. How fortunate for this man that his wife had decided to look in on their old home on the very day that the setting was right for her to ask if the house was being haunted. Perhaps if the wife had never retuned, or if she had not asked, the ghost would still be there, playing music and drilling holes in the furniture of the new residents.

8

Copper Creek & Deep River Mine Shaft

Gold Rush Victims

> "Make money your god and it will plague you like the devil."
> -- *Henry Fielding (1707–1754)*

Most people when they think of a gold rush think of California and imagine what it was like back in the late 1840s and early 1850s. They think of the gold seekers popularly called "forty-niners," the Sutter's Mill incident, and Pike's Peak. They begin to subconsciously sing the American folk ballad "Oh, My Darling, Clementine."

Jamestown, named in honor of James Mendenhall in 1816 (see "Mendenhall Plantation" section), was largely a Quaker settlement. Gold had been discovered there reportedly as early back as 1800. And yet, no one ever thinks of Jamestown, North Carolina, and its gold rush. In fact, many gold mining techniques utilizing the newest bit of technology known as the steam engine were developed and perfected by Cornish engineers Charles McCulloch and Elizer Kersey. In 1832 they opened McCulloch Gold Mill that was a key

Chapter Eight

part of the state's gold mining industry, until, in 1849, miners began moving out west to California.

"Castle" McCulloch, as it was called because of its castle-like appearance, drawbridge, and vaulted ceilings, next saw interest when it briefly served as a field hospital during the Civil War. Eventually the castle was purchased and restored to its original beautiful self during the 1980s. These days the castle hosts more wedding receptions than would-be "forty-niners."

Jamestown, back in the days when it was a gold mining town, had to have had its fair share of accidents and deaths. Oddly, I was only able to find two that had a ghost story connected to them. I thought that I would include them both here because Jamestown is home to a little over 3,000 people. It's a small community and I can't help but imagine that just about everyone in the town frequents the city of Greensboro to shop, work, or seek entertainment. And when they do so, they all have to pass right under Lydia's Bridge (see "Lydia's Bridge" section).

The first Jamestown Gold Rush ghost tale takes place in an old rock house. This is the building where the ore would be sorted by hand and then smelted. The story goes on to say that a slave working in this one rock house had something of a disagreement with his foreman. The slave was pushed or perhaps even backing up of his own volition, but in either event, he fell through a huge glass window and landed, head first, on the craggy rocks below in Copper Creek.

The years passed and the names of the slave, his boss, and even the mining company itself have been forgotten. What have remained, however, are the bloodstains on the rocks. Folks who report seeing them say they look fresh.

The other Gold Rush ghost story I discovered happened in the Deep River Mine Shaft. The story here is that a sudden and violent argument broke out between two miners. Fights over claim jumping were common, but this one ended in death. One of the participants cut a rope that the other was using at the time, causing him to plummet to his demise. It is said that if you go to the mine shaft

Copper Creek & Deep River Mine Shaft

today, if you're lucky (from a certain point of view), you will be able to hear the screaming descent and sudden silencing crash of the man who fell to his death.

†††††††††††††

The Jamestown Historical Society is located at 603 West Main Street in Jamestown, North Carolina. For further information, call 336-454-3819, Eastern Standard Time.

Castle McCulloch is located at 6000 Kersey Valley Road, Jamestown, North Carolina. Please visit the Web site for a full list of special events and operating hours at www.castlemcculloch.com. For further information please call 336-887-5413.

†††††††††††††

9

Dana Auditorium

> "I think I should have no other mortal wants, if I could always have plenty of music. It seems to infuse strength into my limbs and ideas into my brain. Life seems to go on without effort, when I am filled with music."
> -- *George Eliot (1819–1880)*

Guilford College Campus

Ever since its construction was completed, there have been curious goings-on at Dana Auditorium. It may have something to do with the fact that this particular Guilford College building was built directly on top of what is believed to be the area where the field hospital was during the Battle of Guilford Courthouse of the Revolutionary War (see "Guilford Courthouse National Military Park" section). Many people subscribe to the idea that ghosts are "created" at places where there is much suffering and death. If there is any truth to this, then it is small wonder that there are not more ghosts at Dana other than the well-known "Lucas."

"Lucas," as he has come to be called, is most often experienced by security guards at night in either the Moon Room or the Choir Room. Public Safety Officer Rhonda Johnson told me herself of some of the strange goings-on. She said that at night when the guards lock up, all the lights are turned off, but by the time they leave and lock the front

Dana Auditorium

door behind them, a light or two is seen burning. Johnson said that on one frustrating occasion it took the guards four attempts to turn off all the lights and lock the door successfully. In the end, they decided to let Lucas win.

In the Choir room, there are numerous pianos. It is said of all the pianos in the room that Lucas prefers the one that is on the slightly elevated platform. Guards have often reported that they can hear the tinkling of keys as they approach, but when they reach the door, all music suddenly stops.

Guards also say that they sometimes feel as if someone is following them as they do their rounds. One guard described it as a cold tingling feeling, a lot like fear, but more titillating.

Chapter Nine

Clearly marked on a neat and well-maintained campus is a sign for Dana Auditorium. The Moon Room is where a ghostly man is seen walking the halls, passing through walls, and thoroughly frightening those who see him.

Near the Moon Room, a ghostly man described as wearing a trench coat and a weathered hat pulled down over his head has been sighted. When a guard called out to him, the figure turned and *walked through* a wall into the Moon Room. Set up much like a chapel these days, it has muted yellow walls with crisp white trim, neat lines of pews, a humble podium, and a modest organ. The Moon Room is about the furthest thing one would think of when imagining a haunted room.

Dana Auditorium

In regards to the ghost seen wearing the long trench coat and hat, I personally feel that he is not connected to the Battle of Guilford Courthouse. I say this only because historically, there was no rain the two days before or after the battle. Assuming of course that he was wearing this outfit when he died, he sounds to me, based on his description, that he was dressed for rainy weather.

As the guards do their nightly patrol outside the auditorium, they also claim to see a light turned on in the Moon or Choir Rooms. However, when they enter the building and go to the rooms, they discover that the lights have already been turned off. And, in many instances, the doors are firmly locked.

Two guards were reported as actually being present in the room on the night when the large chandelier in the auditorium fell. They claim to have seen it begin to sway back and forth, gaining momentum until it finally broke free and crashed into several rows of seating.

A quiet and humble room, the Moon Room shows no traces whatsoever of being haunted. Most often used as a chapel, I found this beautiful yellow room with white trimming to have a certain serenity about it.

Chapter Nine

Even Public Safety Officer Rhonda Johnson has had a strange event happen to her in there. She claims that while walking down the aisle she felt what could only be described as a spider web sticking across her face, as if she had just walked through it. It seemed unlikely that she did. Had there been a spider web present, it would have been destroyed when she first walked up the aisle. Also, the width of the room, at least one hundred feet, just seems to be too vast a distance for a regional spider to make a web across that quickly. To be certain, there are spiders that are large web builders, but webs of that size are usually easy for the human eye to see and the human being to avoid.

Most interesting about the hauntings is that they all seem to occur at or around two o'clock in the morning. Perhaps this was the time of death of the ghost we call Lucas.

†††††††††††††††

Dana Auditorium is located on the Guilford College Campus. If you're heading up Friendly Avenue, turn left onto the road leading into the campus before you reach the traffic light at the corner where Friendly meets New Garden Road. On campus, Dana will be ahead on the right. Lucas is somewhere within.

†††††††††††††††

10

The Devil's Tramping Ground

> "It is the greatest art of the devil to convince us he does not exist."
> *Charles Baudelaire (1821–1867)*

The Devil's Tramping Ground is not located in Greensboro, but rather in Siler City, about thirty-five miles southeast. While I know it's not in Greensboro, and therefore not technically a *Haunted Historic Greensboro* location, I chose to include it here for a couple of reasons.

First of all, the Devil's Tramping Ground is something of a local favorite as far as haunted places go. So many people in the area know of it, have been there, or at the very least, have heard something creepy about it. In fact, a good number of folks I spoke to while doing this book have been there or have first-hand knowledge of someone who has been.

Another reason to include it in the book is because it's such a well-known site with a number of reported incidents that to leave it out without so much as a mention would somehow seem unprofessional.

But I suppose the main reason I decided to include it in the book was because of the people I interviewed along the way. After all, the 240,000 residents of the city of Greensboro can't all be wrong.

Although all the stories regarding the Tramping Ground are virtually all the same, the consistency and persistence of the tales

Chapter Ten

have struck a dark chord in the hearts of anyone who will listen to the tales.

Literally, for centuries, people have been talking about this little patch of earth. The very first "official" report about Devil's Tramping Ground was written in a 1746 surveyor's report describing the clearing and its compacted earth. H. T. Ivy penned the next documented write up in 1882 for *The Morning Star* newspaper out of Wilmington, North Carolina in which he described the area. Then, in the January 2, 1898 edition of Siler City's *The Messenger*, James I. Morris wrote about the hometown haunt.

In the 1800s, when settlers first came to the area, they found what was described as a cleared circular patch of ground, about forty feet in

The Devil's Tramping Ground

diameter, in which *no plant would grow, no dog would enter into, and no horse would come near*. The foot-wide path that leads up to the circle held the same properties, but with an additional haunting trait: *Any item left on the trail at night would not be found there when the sun rose in the morning.*

Early settlers initially believed that perhaps it was some sort of an Indian burial ground or other type of sacred place where magical rituals that they did not understand were held. The farmers had wanted to believe that the ground was bare due to the fact that for years previous the ritualistic stomping dance of the Native Americans had worn the ground bare. Albeit sound, their theory did not account for why the patch of earth would spook off animals, or cause items to disappear, or never be reclaimed by the forest and sprout new growth. What it did do, however, was take on a life of its own.

This is another of the many paths off Devil's Tramping Ground Road. As you can see in the photo, this particular path has a felled tree that is acting as a bridge. Just on the other side of that crop of trees is where one of the alleged "real" Tramping Ground locations is said to be.

Chapter Ten

This is where we parked our car. If you are facing this road, spin on your heal and look across the street. There, you will see a break in the tree line and a path. That path is the trail that leads to the Devil's Tramping Ground. The "forbidden road" shown here is so wide and obviously well used, I honestly wonder if large-scale construction equipment was used to make it. And if they were, I wonder if houses are going to be built there. And if they are, I further wonder if prospective buyers will be alerted to the fact that their potential new home is sitting a stone's throw from a famous haunted locale. North Carolina state law does demand total and full disclosure of a property's history. I can't imagine anyone from North Carolina, let alone Siler City, not being aware of where their new house is built. Especially if they forget to change the name of the road from "Devil's Tramping Ground."

Tales of the cleared circular patch began to grow and spread. It was said that none other than Lucifer himself made the path and the circle. That of all the places on the planet he could visit, he chose this spot in Siler City to appear in and pace upon every night while thinking up new and even more mischievous ways to corrupt mankind and trick men into damning their souls.

As far as my research could tell me, every generation has a "great tale" about someone who spent some part of the night either on the path to or in the circle itself. Also, I noticed, that about every other Halloween

The Devil's Tramping Ground

it is mentioned in the papers, along with other haunted locations, such as Lydia and her bridge (see "Lydia's Bridge" section).

The general story of the Tramping Ground goes like this:

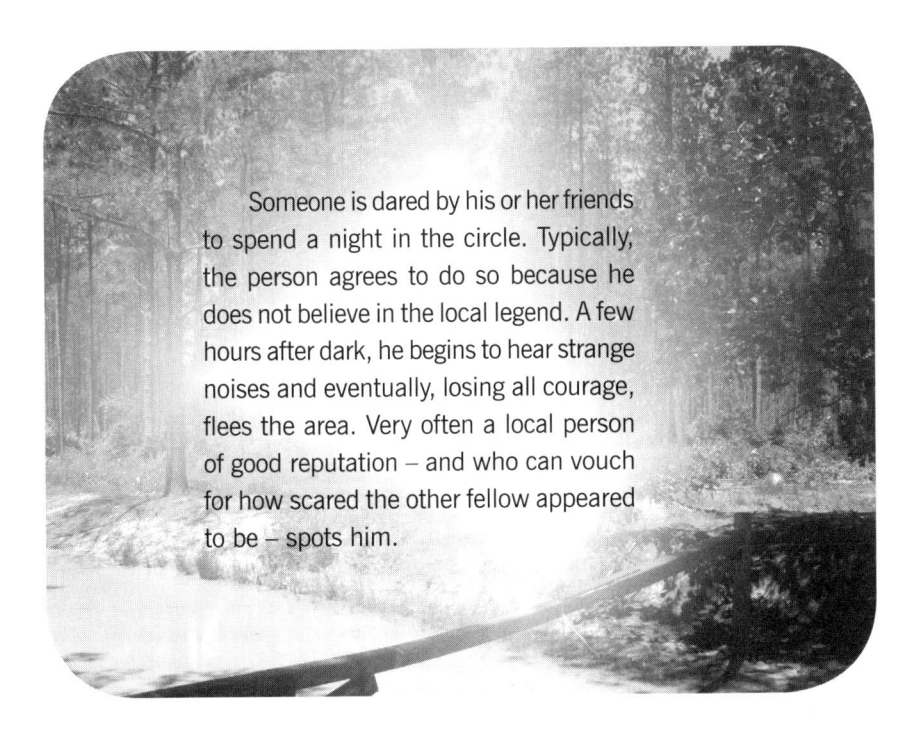

> Someone is dared by his or her friends to spend a night in the circle. Typically, the person agrees to do so because he does not believe in the local legend. A few hours after dark, he begins to hear strange noises and eventually, losing all courage, flees the area. Very often a local person of good reputation – and who can vouch for how scared the other fellow appeared to be – spots him.

I met and spoke with several folks who claimed that as a kid they camped out down there, got spooked, and fled; or placed something on the trail because they were too afraid to actually spend the night, and upon returning in the morning, saw that—much to their surprise and fearful delight—the item that was placed on the trail was gone. The scariest story I was told, in my humble opinion, came from a friend whose family is from the area. She told me that her father, while on maneuvers with his army unit, had camped in the circle. In the morning he and several others awoke to find that they had all been moved several feet to the left.

In fact, there was much to-do made about Devil's Tramping Ground that back in the 1950s, amid the UFO craze that was sweeping the nation, the North Carolina Department of Agriculture decided to see if there was any truth to the centuries-old stories of the Tramping Ground.

Chapter Ten

One more picture of yet another path that wanders off into the woods, and it looks virtually identical to a half dozen more just like it. It too, like the others on the road, is well worn and has what I suspect to be the tracks of a four-wheeler. The only thing truly notable about this path in particular is that this is the one that some folks claim goes to the real Tramping Ground.

They sent a field team to the site to take soil samples to determine what was causing the infertility inside the perfectly formed circle while right outside of it grass grew lush and green.

Accordingly, it was reported in many sources that I happened upon that there was "exceptionally high levels of sodium chloride" inside the circle and on the path. Outside the circle, these same sources claimed, the land was healthy.

I was skeptical every time I would come across this bit of information because it cited an official government report. Yet, in all the sources that cited this NCDA report, not one of them gave anything that was what I would consider to be "reliable or traceable information." For instance, none of the sources named a single scientist who worked on the project, a lab where the soil was tested, or even so much as the exact year the test was done. It seemed to me that if this report existed and anyone had ever seen it, they would have

The Devil's Tramping Ground

mentioned something notable about it, like a file number or some other identifying or researchable fact.

I wanted to know for myself if the test was ever taken or if the report even existed. I have made numerous calls to the North Carolina Department of Agriculture to see how I could go about obtaining a written copy of that soil sample report.

Most of the people I spoke with at the NCDA had never heard of such a report being done, although they had heard of the Devil's Tramping Ground. A few employees even commented that it would be a good idea to conduct such a test. I was also told that if the test *was* done back in the 1950s that the original report was long gone. Generally speaking, I was told that the reports themselves were not kept, but rather a summation consisting of one or two lines would have been created and entered into their annual log. This technique was used, I was told, because even back then the state did about 336,000 soil samples per year.

There was another important bit of information that was explained to me: that in all likelihood the report did not exist. What seemed to be the most reliable bit of evidence to explain the reason behind the clearing was the very thing that was its undoing. Apparently, the language that was being quoted as having been lifted directly from the report, phrases such as "exceptionally high levels," would never have been used in an official state report, especially back then. The NCDA is for the most part a conservative institution and would not use flowery statements of sentiment or hyperbole to make a point, no matter how extreme. Phrases like "higher than expected levels" would have been used no matter how high the levels were, so long as they were not dangerously high, toxic, or posed a public threat.

And just as I had about convinced myself that there never had been a report, that other writers before me had cited sources before them all the way back to an original fraud, I received a phone call from the NCDA's Dr. Colleen Hudak-Wise. As it happened, she told me that Dr. Hardy, Section Chief of the Agronomic Department, claimed not only to remember the report, but that he has the original still, buried somewhere in his office.

It was then promised to me in a phone conversation that a copy of the report would be sent to me after it was found, but, as of this

Chapter Ten

writing, I'm still waiting to receive a copy of it. Yes, I've made numerous follow-up calls. And yes, I have sent my request to them in writing, using both e-mail and the tried-and-true traditional post. If the day ever comes that I do receive it, I will happily post it on my personal Web site, www.theresabane.com, under the heading "Devil's Tramping Ground: Original 1950's Soil Sample Report" for future researchers to see and cite for themselves.

What I do have however are three soil sample reports that were collected by Soil Scientist Rich Hayes who works with the North Carolina Division of Water Quality in the Department of Environment and Natural Resources (DWQ-DENR). This is the state agency that is responsible for regulating and protecting ground and surface water. In fact, he sent me theses reports himself.

Back in the late fall of 2000, Hayes was contacted by a television production company that was planning a show highlighting mysterious events and locations. The show, which sadly never aired, approached him not only for his knowledge and expertise in soil sampling readings, but also because he was the Project Leader of the Chatham County Soil Survey that was happening at that time. Hayes has worked in his field for over twenty years and has taken over 100,000 samples from various locations all over the state of North Carolina.

For the show, Hayes took samples from three different locations: one from the surrounding forest, one from the path, and one from inside the circle itself. These samples were then sent off to the NCDA&CS to be tested. What follows are the reports, in their entirety for everyone to see. As far I'm aware, in all the books I have poured through gathering and collecting information, this book, the one you are holding in your hands right now, is the only published book to ever show the actual results for soil samples that have been taken from the Devil's Tramping Ground.

Soil Sample TBSC1 shows the results from the soil taken from the center of the circle. As you can clearly see in the area labeled "Agronomist" that Dr. M. Ray Tucker, who at the time was the Section Chief of the Soil Testing Agronomic Division, has made a rather curious response: "This one is a mystery." Let me put the conspiracy theorist to rest—the comment was in answer to a direct question posed to Tucker by Hayes. Back when originally approached by the TV production

The Devil's Tramping Ground

company, Hayes had informed Tucker that he was taking soil samples to be tested and asked his fellow colleague for his personal opinion on the matter. Although this is an official state test it was not initiated by

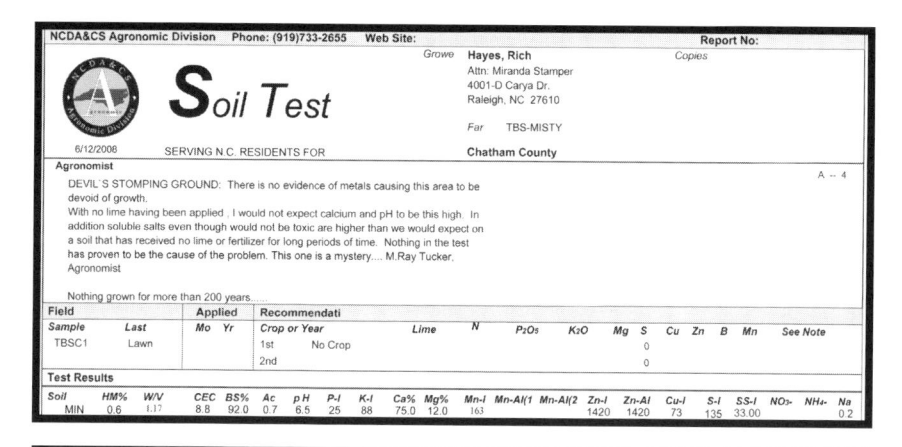

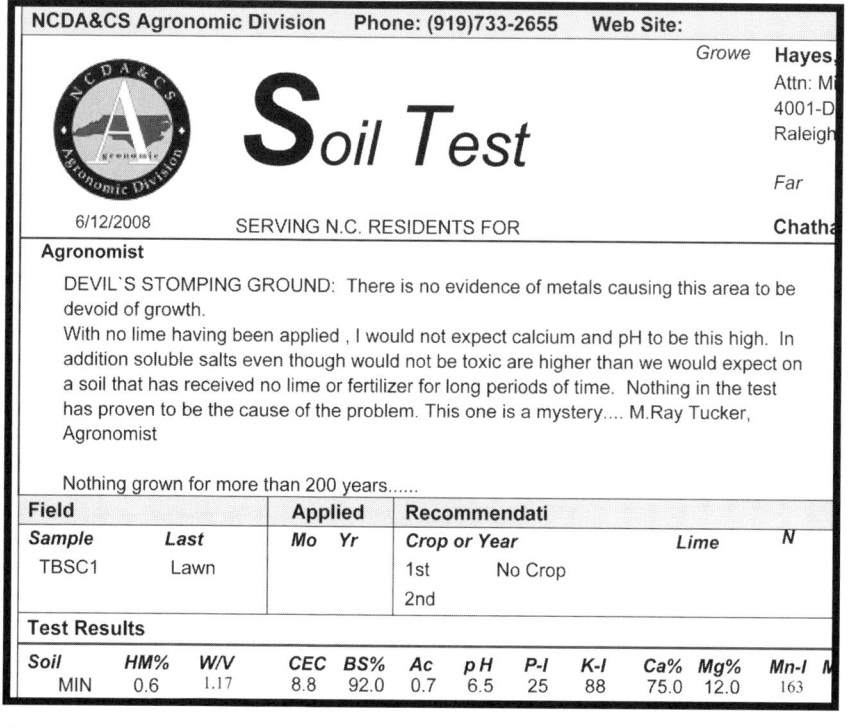

NCDA&CS Agronomic Division   Phone: (919)733-2655   Web Site: Report No:

Growe Hayes, Rich
Attn: Miranda Stamper
4001-D Carya Dr.
Raleigh, NC 27610

Far   TBS-MISTY

6/12/2008   SERVING N.C. RESIDENTS FOR   Chatham County

Soil Test

Agronomist

DEVIL'S STOMPING GROUND: There is no evidence of metals causing this area to be devoid of growth.
With no lime having been applied, I would not expect calcium and pH to be this high. In addition soluble salts even though would not be toxic are higher than we would expect on a soil that has received no lime or fertilizer for long periods of time. Nothing in the test has proven to be the cause of the problem. This one is a mystery.... M.Ray Tucker, Agronomist

Nothing grown for more than 200 years......

Field		Applied		Recommendati										
Sample	Last	Mo	Yr	Crop or Year		Lime	N	P_2O_5	K_2O	Mg	S	Cu	Zn	B	Mn	See Note
TBSC1	Lawn			1st	No Crop						0					
				2nd							0					

Test Results

Soil	HM%	W/V	CEC	BS%	Ac	pH	P-I	K-I	Ca%	Mg%	Mn-I	Mn-Al(1	Mn-Al(2	Zn-I	Zn-Al	Cu-I	S-I	SS-I	NO_3-	NH_4-	Na
MIN	0.6	1.17	8.8	92.0	0.7	6.5	25	88	75.0	12.0	163			1420	1420	73	135	33.00			0.2

This is a scan of the first of three official documents that the NCDA&CS sent to me. It has been titled by the state as TBSC1. This document shows the results for the soil sample that was taken from the center of the infamous circle.

Chapter Ten

Soil Test — NCDA&CS Agronomic Division   Phone: (919)733-2655   Web Site:

Growe Hayes, Rich
Attn: Miranda Stamper
4001-D Carya Dr.
Raleigh, NC 27610

Far

6/12/2008   SERVING N.C. RESIDENTS FOR   Chatham County

Agronomist

Soil pH is much lower than desired for the sample area. Apply the recommended lime below and incorporate into the soil for best results. Phosphorus and potassium are adequate for the sample area. Sulfur is marginal for the sample.

T. Kent Yarborough, Agronomist

Field Sample	Last	Applied Mo Yr	Recommendati Crop or Year	Lime	N	P₂O₅	K₂O	Mg	S	Cu	Zn	B	Mn	See Note
TBSP1			1st Fes/OG/Tim,E	1.2T	50-70	0	0	0	0	0	0	.0	0	12
			2nd Fes/OG/Tim,	0	120-200	0	0	0	0	0	0	.0	0	12

Test Results

Soil	HM%	W/V	CEC	BS%	Ac	pH	P-I	K-I	Ca%	Mg%	Mn-I	Mn-Al(1	Mn-Al(2	Zn-I	Zn-Al	Cu-I	S-I	SS-I	NO₃-	NH₄-	Na
MIN	0.37	1.18	3.7	65.0	1.3	4.6	101	136	38.0	10.0	48	38	38	57	57	54	28	11.00			0.1

NCDA&CS Agronomic Division   Phone: (919)733-2655   Web Site:

Growe Hayes,
Attn: M
4001-D
Raleigh

Far

6/12/2008   SERVING N.C. RESIDENTS FOR   Chatha

Soil Test

Agronomist

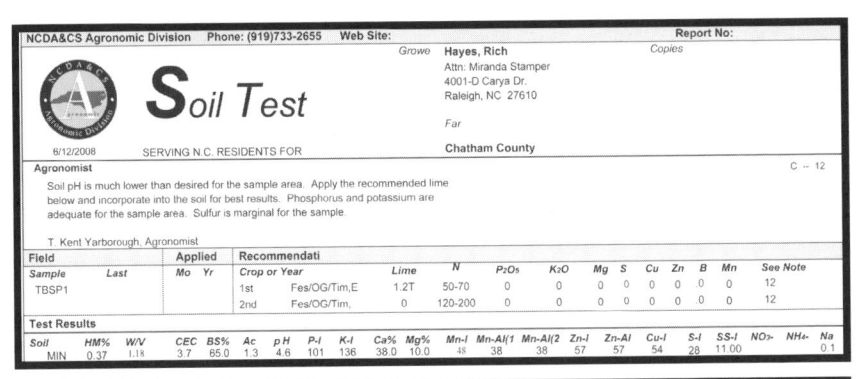

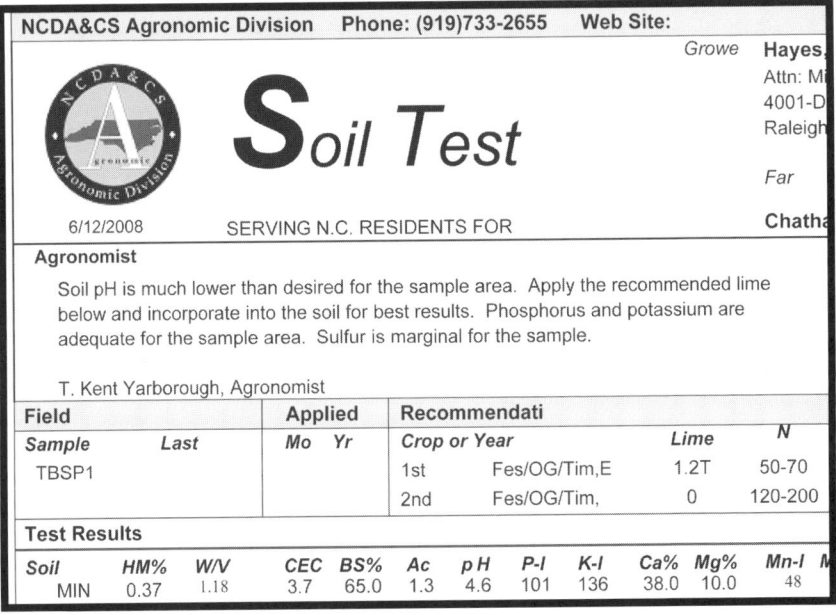

Soil pH is much lower than desired for the sample area. Apply the recommended lime below and incorporate into the soil for best results. Phosphorus and potassium are adequate for the sample area. Sulfur is marginal for the sample.

T. Kent Yarborough, Agronomist

Field Sample	Last	Applied Mo Yr	Recommendati Crop or Year	Lime	N
TBSP1			1st Fes/OG/Tim,E	1.2T	50-70
			2nd Fes/OG/Tim,	0	120-200

Test Results

Soil	HM%	W/V	CEC	BS%	Ac	pH	P-I	K-I	Ca%	Mg%	Mn-I
MIN	0.37	1.18	3.7	65.0	1.3	4.6	101	136	38.0	10.0	48

This document has been named TBSP1 and shows the results for the soil that was taken from the "path" of the Tramping Ground. The notes made by the Agronomist in this area is more along the lines of how I expect a government form to read. It appears that the number representing the mineral breakdown for the path is for the most part, close to the numbers for the "forest" sample.

the state, and therefore the casualness of the language is explained as nothing more than friendly banter between two coworkers.

Hayes told me about the soil samples he had taken. First, he said that the land that makes up the pathway and the circle are areas of compacted earth. Invisible to the eye, you can clearly feel the difference when you're walking on it. Normally there is some level of give to ground,

The Devil's Tramping Ground

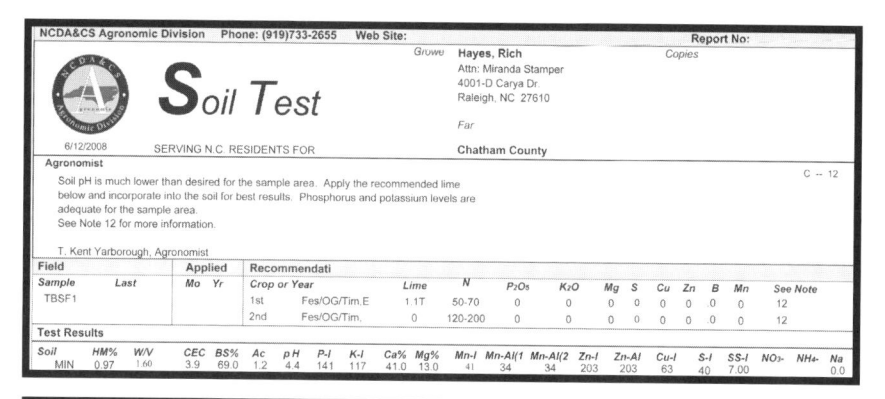

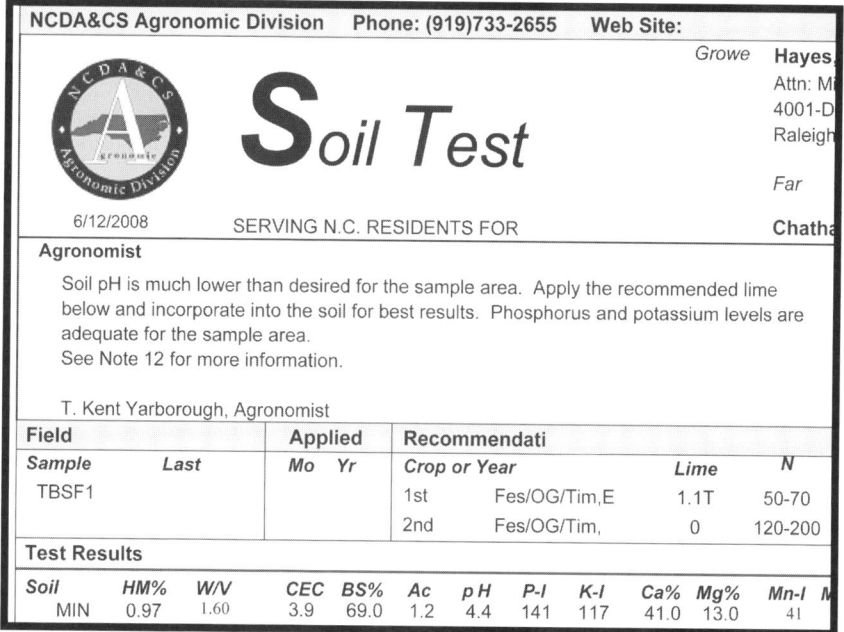

Field			Applied		Recommendati											
Sample	Last		Mo	Yr	Crop or Year		Lime	N	P₂O₅	K₂O	Mg	S	Cu	Zn	B	Mn	See Note
TBSF1					1st Fes/OG/Tim,E		1.1T	50-70	0	0	0	0	0	0	.0	0	12
					2nd Fes/OG/Tim,		0	120-200	0	0	0	0	0	0	.0	0	12

Test Results

Soil	HM%	W/V	CEC	BS%	Ac	pH	P-I	K-I	Ca%	Mg%	Mn-I	Mn-Al(1	Mn-Al(2	Zn-I	Zn-Al	Cu-I	S-I	SS-I	NO₃-	NH₄-	Na
MIN	0.97	1.60	3.9	69.0	1.2	4.4	141	117	41.0	13.0	41	34	34	203	203	63	40	7.00			0.0

(Soil Test report from NCDA&CS Agronomic Division, dated 6/12/2008, for Hayes, Rich, Chatham County. Agronomist note: "Soil pH is much lower than desired for the sample area. Apply the recommended lime below and incorporate into the soil for best results. Phosphorus and potassium levels are adequate for the sample area. See Note 12 for more information." — T. Kent Yarborough, Agronomist)

This document has been named TBSF1 and shows the results for the test preformed on what would appear to be the healthy and thriving forested area immediately outside of the Devil's Tramping Ground.

and we can all agree that there is a marked difference when walking on cement and a front lawn. Hayes said that the compacted earth of the path more so than the circle is very hard, so much so that it is difficult to even work a shovel into.

Hayes said that the area itself is somewhat unique. When last he was in the area, what struck him as most odd was the lack of sapling

Chapter Ten

pine and sweet gum trees. Normally these species are considered an invasionary species of plant capable of growing en mass, even in the shallowest of soil. The topsoil in the woods around Devil's Tramping Ground goes only about three feet deep before hitting bedrock. But pine and sweet gum are the same species of plant whose little saplings can be seen growing out of the cracks in sidewalks and in the gutters of houses. For that matter, the trees that did manage to mature in the area were notably stunted in their growth. Hayes is interested in why the seeds from the trees in the area are not sprouting new growth.

Going back to the original reports of the Tramping Ground and its inability to support plant life, Hayes was quick to point out that although there are modern day herbicides that can render a patch of earth useless, several hundred years ago, this was not what could have ruined the land. In his professional and scientific opinion, there would have been only three methods back in those days that a person would use to cause infertility in the land: salt, sulphur, and copper.

Referring back to each of the three soil sample reports, you can see for yourself that under the heading "*Na*" that the sodium levels although high are not toxic. In fact, there are numerous places in the state with higher levels of sodium that support plant life just fine.

S-1, or sulphur, was also tested on the report. A reading of 4.6 is about average statewide, but from 6.5 to 7 is not only considered neutral but is in fact ideal for growing vegetables. Scientifically, in theory at least, there is no reason whatsoever why this area is not replete with tomatoes.

The last key factor that could cause vegetation to not grow in an area is the presence of copper, listed as "*Cu-1*" on the report. Copper is a natural sterilization agent. Although there were copper mines in Chatham, Moore, Lee, and Guildford counties at one time, the levels reported on the test do not indicate a level of copper that would prevent growth. Nor were these mines anywhere near the Tramping Ground, so natural run-off is not a possible explanation either. As a metal, copper would not have disintegrated over time or dissolved into the soil. Indeed, it would have been an expensive and pointless practical joke, to take perfectly good copper ore and grind it up into a fine powder and spread it out over a patch of earth that one owned or was using for anything. It would have been a victimless crime, but also an expensive and meaningless one.

The Devil's Tramping Ground

In Hayes professional opinion, there is no scientific reason for the lack of plant life in the area.

Then I spoke to Mr. Perry Wyatt, a retired soil scientist for the NCDENR (North Carolina Department of Environment and Natural Resources). Wyatt agrees that a soil sample will tell you what minerals are in the soil and at what levels, and that he personally has looked at innumerable ones over the course of his career. However, he says that if you know what is in the soil and at what levels, and you still have a problem with plant life not wanting to grow, you need to run a Particle Size Analysis Test. This is key, Wyatt claims, because it will tell you how much silt is in the soil.

Silt, as Wyatt explained to me, is one of the three ingredients that make up soil. He simplified it for me saying that as rock erodes it first breaks down into sand, and that breaks down into an intermediate stage called silt, and that breaks further down into clay. He went on to explain that silt particles under a microscope are shaped very much like dinner dishes. When these particles are stacked on top of one another, they compress very close together and greatly hinder plant growth by impeding the spreading of roots throughout the soil.

It is Wyatt's personal opinion that the area known as Devil's Tramping Ground was once a springtime meeting place for local Indian tribes on their way to the Deep River to fish. He believes that these tribes used the area as a campsite and the constant traffic caused the silt particles to stack upon one another tightly, an act the particles are quicker to do in springtime weather. This traffic made what is known as a *densick layer*, or a compact layer, of earth about six to eight inches beneath the surface.

Professionally, Wyatt will tell you that the only way to reclaim the land would be with extensive and major soil management techniques. This would include deeply tilling up the earth and mixing in more fertile soil.

Personally, I don't see that happening anytime in the near future. The person who owns the property where Devil's Tramping Ground is located inherited it. It's been in the family for some two hundred years, and in all that time, the land has never been used to grow any sort of cash crop. It's more or less now the way it was when it was first reported back in the 1700s.

Of course, after all of this, my faithful assistant Joy and I had to visit this place for ourselves and see if we could experience any sort of otherworldly anything. As terrifying as it would be to actually see the Devil,

Chapter Ten

tall and red and cloven-hoofed perhaps, pacing a circle and mumbling to himself as he plotted the demise of humanity, long pointed tail swishing back and forth in anticipation and frustration, it was also a bit exciting.

Once my delving into research books and scientific papers was finished, the next thing I had learned about Devil's Tramping Ground is that no one I spoke to at first could readily give me directions to it. Even folks who had told me they had been there said it had been years back and were not sure they could give me accurate directions, as all the landmarks they would have been familiar with were long gone. I tell you as they told me: It's down a country road near Harper's Crossroads. That only helps if you know where Harper's Crossroads is, which we didn't, so it was time to look for better directions than that to get us there.

Although you can find on the Internet literal step-by-step driving directions to the Tramping Ground, they are not what I would consider accurate or complete, as I and my faithful assistant Joy tried to follow them. In fact, woefully inadequate and non-functional would be better descriptions. One web site even listed latitude and longitude coordinates that my personal GPS would accept. Sadly, they took us to the Pisgah Covered Bridge in Pisgah, North Carolina, a mere thirty-five miles off the mark. Interesting if you like covered bridges, but a poor substitute for the Tramping Ground.

Dr. Hayes had suggested using "Google Earth," as someone had noted the location of the Tramping Ground on it. What this free downloadable program does is show you any spot on the planet from an aerial view. I tried it using my parent's house in New Jersey as a test. The results were very impressive. The photo must have been taken on a Sunday around dinnertime because I could clearly see both my parents' cars were in the driveway and each of my brothers cars parked in the street. In fact, I was able to zoom in on the area close enough to almost make out a license plate. The program worked equally well when I entered "The Devil's Tramping Ground" in the search window. From the photo you can clearly see, without trespassing at all, that the much talked about circle is in fact a rather amorphous shape, more like an upset stomach. The program also has an option for getting driving directions. With another click of a button you can "fly" there from your computer screen by entering the address of the location from where you are to where you want to go. We entered the information, but we didn't use those directions. Google Earth, as great as it is at this writing, did not have

The Devil's Tramping Ground

the names of the streets on the map as they appear in the real world. For instance: Jones Street, as the actual, physical street sign would read, is listed as SR 3421 on Google Earth. Not entirely helpful.

So, finally, here they are and I share them with you—the tried-and-true working directions to Devil's Tramping Ground. I got them the old fashioned way, from a friendly set of cashiers at a local gas station. These directions work, I promise you; I used them myself to get there.

†††††††††††††††

Assuming of course that you are in the great city of Greensboro, use whatever method you like to get onto I-40 East. Take exit 126 to Sanford and at the bottom of the exit, make a right turn onto Martin Luther King, Jr. Road. This road is also known as 421 South. Continue along this road and take Exit 174, the Piney Grove Church Road exit. Turn right off the exit and go about a mile down the road. At the fork in the road, bear left onto Old 421 North. You'll come to a traffic light at the corner of Highway 64 East and Greensboro Avenue; cross over Highway 64 and take the first left onto North Second Street. At the fourth traffic light, make a right onto East Raleigh Street. It will quickly become West Raleigh Street, and then change names again to Siler City Glendon Road. You'll be on this road for a while, just over six miles, when you come to a flashing caution light. There, make a right turn onto Bonnlee Bennett Road and drive two miles to the first crossroads you come to. At the crossroads, make a left onto a street named, I kid you not, "Devil's Tramping Ground Road." Three miles ahead on the right is a gravel apron immediately blocked by a chain and metal post. This is what everyone told me was the main road that led to the Devil's Tramping Ground. Now, some folks say that it's not—they claim that the real site is on the opposite side of the road on the left, or to the west. Since one of "those folks" was Dr. Richard Hayes who had permission from the owner of the property to go out there and collect soil samples, I am leaning towards believing his opinion on which site is the real site.

†††††††††††††††

Now, in reality, whichever location you believe the Tramping Ground to be, the forty-foot clearing that has been the center of many campfire conversations for the better part of the last two centuries is on private

Chapter Ten

In Siler City, North Carolina, there actually is a road named "Devil's Tramping Ground Road." This state-issued sign is firmly planted in the ground in cement, making me wonder how many times a year the State needs to come by and install a new one. It is by the way, very firmly planted into the ground. The street sign is also about eight feet off the ground and not at all easy to reach. On a side note, I did look up the road name on my GPS and no such road by that name was listed. I suspect that my GPS had it registered as a State Road (SR) and a number.

property. There are numerous "No Trespassing" signs posted on about every other tree and fence post in the entire area. So many signs are posted that there is no way to even accidentally not see them and feign ignorance if you're caught. In fact, in the little while that Joy and I were there looking for any path or walkway that was not marked with a No Trespassing sign, two police cars cruised by at various intervals to see what we were doing.

We parked my car on a patch of newly laid crush rock, just opposite of what I'm assuming to be the real path that leads to the Devil's Tramping Ground. If you had permission to walk the property from the owner, it is only about a mile down a shady, wide, and clear dirt path and then a left turn down the path that leads into the circle.

The Devil's Tramping Ground

I did not walk down any of the dirt roads and into the Tramping Ground itself for a couple of reasons. First and foremost, I did not have permission from the owner to walk the land, and to do so would have been breaking the law. I asked at a local convenience store (where I got the driving directions) if they or anyone they knew could tell me who the legal owner was. All I wanted was permission to look around and take a few pictures. No one knew exactly who owned the land, but I was heavily assured that it would be fine to go ahead and look around. I believed them, but I really did feel uncomfortable about breaking the law. Besides, it was a rather warm and sunny day, and the grass was tall enough to reach my knees. I was certain that once we were in the clearing of the Tramping Ground we would be safe from rattlesnakes; it would have been easy enough to spot their brown bodies against the yellowish ground, if any of them dared to enter into the haunted patch of earth. It was the walk through what could have been snake-infested territory that concerned me most. We truly were out in the country, and far from help should we need it. I decided to err on the side of caution.

From what I could tell, these days neither the Devil nor his Tramping Ground are what they once were. For starters, there is not one well-worn

This is one of the many paths that are located on Devil's Tramping Ground Road. Not only is it much wider than we expected the trail to be, easily ten feet across, it was well marked with "No Trespassing" signs. I suspect that part of the reason nothing grows on the path has to do more with the tire tracks that were visible in the dirt here than anything else.

Chapter Ten

trail heavily posted against trespassing, but perhaps a half dozen off the self-titled main road, each leading to an irregular-shaped clearing with the obvious remains of a campfire. In all certainty, there is no telling which of the trails lead to the real Tramping Ground. All the roads were equally well worn and littered upon, and it being as nice a day as it was when we visited the area, there were plenty of birds out and about, chirping up a storm.

Back at what I was assured was the *real* path, beer bottles and cans of numerous labels are scattered all over. There are more cigarette butts than leaves on the ground. I suspect that if anything is keeping plant life from growth it's all the nicotine leaking into the earth from the cigarette filters. There are also bits of evidence scattered on the ground and down the trail as far as the eye can see that would make every mother's blood run cold: condom wrappers, used prophylactics, and the occasional odd bit of clothing. I seriously doubt that even the Devil himself would have enough time in a single night to clear a path of all the debris.

The largest of the clearings we heard about was a mere seventeen feet across at its irregular widest, a far cry from the much-acclaimed forty feet. I was told this by one person who claimed that he had measured it. This fact he provided me with coincides with an article I had read in a fairly recent book about the Tramping Ground. It also loosely coincided with the aerial shot I was able to study from Google Earth.

But perhaps the most disappointing part of the trip to the much-famed Tramping Ground is that wiregrass grew, albeit thinly, in every clearing, on every trail. Real bright green grass did grow in abundance and shamed the wiregrass that managed to sprout up amidst the shards of glass and cigarette filters, but it did grow. I wish I had been able to secure permission to visit the site because Mr. Wyatt had asked me to pay attention to the trees. He had said that the last time he was there the trees in the area had stunted growth; they were shorter and thinner than trees further out from the circle. He also wondered if there were any signs of saplings growing. There were none on his last visit.

So, as it turns out, the much-cited 1950s NCDA soil sample report was real, did exist at some point, and perhaps one day my request for a copy of it will be fulfilled. However, the Devil seems to have abandoned this little patch of dirt in Siler City to those who would rather drink and chain-smoke and pursue other nocturnal recreations. Maybe his plan worked after all?

11

Private Residence, West Friendly Avenue

> "For most of history, Anonymous was a woman."
> -- *Virginia Woolf (1882–1941)*

About twenty years ago, freelance author and editor Mary Best rented a charming little brick house, but it didn't take long before she, her then husband, and their dog Ziff all noticed *something odd* was going on.

When they first went to look at the little old red brick house, they could tell that there was "something" about the place, but they couldn't quite put their finger on it. It was a feeling that could not be described, but since neither one of them had picked up a "bad" or "evil" vibe from the place, they decided to rent the charming small house.

Before they even moved into the home, there was a sign of things to come. The owner had apparently allowed the landlord to let the house go a little bit in regards to regular maintenance. Houses, particularly when they are not being lived in, need to be maintained. The landlord spent little time at the house, especially when it came to repairing things or even updating, like with a periodic fresh coat of paint. It had been some years since any work had been done to the home, and a new coat of paint is a quick and easy fix to give it a more "homey" feeling.

Chapter Eleven

Since the couple was interested in doing the job themselves, they were quickly given the go-ahead.

One day, before the couple moved in, Mary's husband was in the house alone painting one of the rooms. Suddenly, there was the sound of rushing wind running through the house, as if all the air were being pulled out through some great, unseen vacuum. Windows and doors were opening and closing as the wild currents of air raced past them. It stopped as suddenly as it began, and without any delay, Mary's husband ran out.

After they moved in, odd little occurrences continued to happen. The VCR would turn itself on and run tapes forward and backward. The clock in the kitchen behaved oddly as well. No matter what time it was set correctly on, as soon as it was left alone, it would consistently stop at 9:10. Lights all throughout the house would turn themselves on or off. On a few occasions they even thought that they saw a shadowy figure pass by the attic window. Any one of these things happening is spooky on its own, but *ALL* of them happening—and happening fairly regularly at that—was downright scary.

Even Ziff the dog was acting weird. The normally brave and protective shepherd mix acted skittish in the new home, particularly near the door to the basement. On several occasions Mary tried to lure Ziff down there, but with no success. She even moved Ziff's

Friendly Avenue

food bowl to the basement, but the dog would not go down the stairs, not even to eat. There was nothing wholly remarkable about the basement, except perhaps for the stairs. The steps were old and creaked when used as one might expect steps to do in an old house, but there were burn marks apparent on them. No one gave it too much thought at the time; it was, after all, an older house in need of some TLC repairs. It was just assumed that over the years accidents happened there, and one of them obviously left some burn marks on the basement steps.

Mary kept putting Ziff's food near the basement door, and he kept being funny about eating it. Then one day Mary noticed Ziff standing in the kitchen looking at the door with his head cocked to the side. Quietly she snuck up to the doorway and watched her dog seemingly interact with someone she could not see. He bounced up and down on his front legs, bowed down with his rear high in the air, his tail wagging happily back and forth. Then he trotted most triumphantly over to his food bowl and ate without incident. Whatever *it* was that had been bothering Ziff about the basement, he had apparently made a sort of peace with it—and *IT* with him.

Early one October Saturday morning, Mary was in the basement doing laundry. Ziff was down there with her, comfortably sitting and enjoying himself as he watched her work. She was hanging shirts on hangers as they came out of the dryer to prevent them from wrinkling. As she neared the end of her chore, she realized that she had three shirts left to hang but only two hangers. She made a mental note to herself not to forget to go upstairs and get another hanger. Then, suddenly, a great rush of wind swept past her, up the stairs, and through the house. It created a vacuum as it went, forcing doors and windows to open and close. It was an event exactly like the one her husband had described happening to him. As unexpectedly as it started, it stopped. Mary was frozen with fear for several long moments. Eventually, she allowed herself to look around, eyes darting back and forth. She spotted Ziff hiding under the stairs. As she continued to glance around the room, she automatically began inventorying her surroundings. She found the shirt she still needed to hang, and right next to it, at her feet was an extra hanger.

Chapter Eleven

Despite all of the odd goings-on, Mary said that she never felt truly afraid or scared to the point where she felt in danger while she lived there, although she did feel that indescribable and persistent "something." But, as one friend had commented to her about what could only be a ghost, "How bad could it be? It helps out with the laundry."

Six months later, on New Year's Day, Mary and her husband were out for a walk enjoying the weather when they happened across their next-door neighbors, an elderly couple. It was during that casual conversation that Mary discovered the secret of her home.

Apparently, many years ago a couple owned the home. The husband had tried not once, but twice, to kill his wife. For his first attempt, he had tried to kill her by setting the basement steps on fire while she was in the basement. His plan may have well worked, but he had closed the door to the basement, unknowingly cutting off the supply of oxygen that fire needs to burn and spread.

The wife survived, and why she remained with her husband is a mystery. Perhaps he was able to convince her it was an accident, or that he would change his ways. Whatever the reason was that she remained with him in that house, it would prove to be the death of them both.

The husband's second attempt was far more successful. He went into the home's dining room and called her to him. As soon as she was in the room, he shot her and without any hesitation, and then he turned the gun on himself. The husband died instantly, but the wife was found and rushed to Moses Cone Hospital, just down the street. The wife, although she initially survived the gunshot, was rendered completely paralyzed. She was moved to a rest home and died there about two years later.

It was after learning the facts of the case that Mary was able to name what she had been feeling all this time: a female presence. She started calling the spirit "Essie" and counted her as one of the family. Even the neighbors who told them the story claimed to have seen Essie passing by the windows and turning the lights on and off inside the house when they knew the couple was out of town.

12

Guilford Courthouse National Military Park

> "It is not unseemly for a man to die fighting in defense of his country. The single best augury is to fight for one's country."
> -- *Homer (850 BC)*

If you've ever seen the Mel Gibson movie *The Patriot,* you've seen a loose interpretation of the events that led up to a Hollywood reexamination of the historic Battle of Guilford Courthouse. The movie that basically touched upon all the major points will have you believe that the Colonial Army won that battle, but in truth, we did not. Technically, the victory went to the British, but at a heavy cost.

At this time, the rebellious colonists had been able to stalemate the British government and stall the war. The war in the North was deadlocked, neither side able to gain and maintain an advantage. The ranks of the American army were beginning to fill out. France, bitter after losing its colonies in the Seven Year War, made an alliance with the fledgling United States government. British nobleman Sir Henry Clinton had been secretly ordered by King George to retake the American South, thinking that it would be an easy task since it was not as densely populated as the northern colonies. All of these happenings were the catalyst that set the stage for the bloody conflict that would follow.

By May of 1780 Clinton had reclaimed Georgia and South Carolina. The loss of these states was painful to the Americans, but losing

Chapter Twelve

Charleston and her 5,000 defenders, the largest organized body of American troops, was a serious blow to both the war effort and to the freedom fighters' morale.

A month later Clinton received word that the French ships promised to the American army had set sail. Clinton had assumed that the ships were bound for New York harbor and feeling the war in the South was well on its way to being over, decided to return to his northern headquarters. Lord Charles Cornwallis was placed in command by Clinton and given general instructions on how to proceed rather than strict military orders. Clinton felt that so long as Charleston was maintained under British control and a series of outposts established, Cornwallis could move at his discretion into North Carolina and thereafter take Virginia.

Cornwallis started off good; he ordered the construction of the required outposts with the hopes that by doing so would ensure South

Guilford Courthouse National Military Park

Carolina's official succession from the fledgling government. This was not the case, however, as he faced a constant and bloody resistance through a series of guerilla-styled assaults. Cornwallis became increasingly convinced that the best way to secure South Carolina under British rule was to invade North Carolina. It was his opinion that it was a place of safety for partisans, a staging ground for the enemy, largely populated with loyal British colonists wanting to be rescued from the rebel forces, and where the American General Gate was rebuilding his army after a devastating and humiliating recent defeat. Cornwallis further believed that because of Gate's utter failure in his last campaign, he would be replaced, most likely, by someone less qualified and experienced.

Nathanael Greene was chosen personally by the Commander in Chief, General George Washington, to be the new commanding general of the Continental Army's Southern Department. Greene, a Quaker, used every bit of his guile and aggressive nature to wield his smaller and less experienced men. In doing so, he and his army led the British general on a four-month madcap chase across the Carolinas from December of 1780 to March of 1781.

Greene eventually chose the hamlet of Guilford Courthouse to meet Cornwallis. With the recent addition of fresh troops and reinforcements from the Virginia militia, Greene was ready to meet his overly aggressive and well-matched opponent.

Cornwallis camped his men on the Dan River, a mere twelve miles away from the enemy. The British general opted not to attack the Continentals in the middle of the night, which would have heavily demoralized his enemy. Rather he roused his men in the early hours of the day and marched them all morning and into the early afternoon down The Great Road, which we now call New Garden Road here in Greensboro.

The British army first engaged the enemy around 12:30 in the afternoon. Canons were set on The Great Road with the first line of men, militia mostly, who were asked to hold the line only long enough to get off two rounds. They held and fired upon the enemy. Greene's men some miles off in the distance could hear the return gunfire of the British troops and continued to hear the first line hold for nearly an hour.

Around 1:15 the second line of Greene's men engaged the enemy. They met not in the wide-open clearings that the first line had, but

Chapter Twelve

rather in the heavy underbrush of the surrounding woods. Cornwallis's limited cavalry was rendered virtually useless due to the thick Carolina underbrush, as were the bayonets of the soldiers' long rifles. The fighting was close, fierce, and bloody, but eventually, the British broke free and into the next clearing around 2:15 to meet Greene's third and final line. This is where his finest and most elite soldiers stood. They were fully rested and prepared to meet the British army who were hungry, hot, and tired. The Redcoats had either been marching or fighting since dawn and even they could see their numbers dropping with each and every push forward.

This is the famous equestrian statue of General Greene that is located on part of what is referred to as The Third Line. Although this is where the most brutal part of the battle was fought—and also where the mass graves are said to have been dug—most of the battlefield has been converted into apartment complexes and residential housing. This is also the area of the park from where many of the ghost stories are said to originate.

Guilford Courthouse National Military Park

But eventually, the better-equipped, better-disciplined, and more experienced British soldiers began to reconvene. They captured Greene's field artillery and met the enemy in many places on the battlefield in hand-to-hand combat. The fighting at this point was so fierce and so horrific that General Cornwallis himself commanded his artillery crews to load the cannons with grape shot and shoot into the men. He was fully aware that he would hit his own soldiers as well as the enemy, but felt it was the kinder fate to all involved. (Grape shot is a canvas bag filled with small pieces of scrap metal that when fired from a gun or cannon will savage through anything or anyone it meets.)

Eventually the British army broke through and Greene was forced to withdraw. He marched his regiment some fifteen miles away. Overall, he was proud of how well his army had fought, but was deeply upset that he had lost the battle. Of his 4,400 men, he had lost only 268.

Unbeknownst to Greene at that time, Cornwallis was not at all pleased with the outcome. Although he had won the battle, his well-disciplined and experienced British soldiers had taken a proverbial and literal beating from the Continental army. Of the eight hundred men who died that day, 532 of them were from Cornwallis's original 1,924, a staggering twenty-seven percent of his army. Later, when asked about the battle, Cornwallis is quoted as having said, "I never saw such fighting since God made me. The Americans fought like demons."

The Battle of Guilford County Courthouse was a virtual blood bath. The British soldiers who had won the field had also won the right to collect up those who were injured and see to their medical needs. That night the anguished cries of the wounded and dying saw to it that no one was able to sleep. In the morning, the British soldiers who had rations left ate and then were ordered to begin digging mass graves to bury the dead. Bodies were everywhere over the thousands-acre battlefield. After the dead were buried en masse in unmarked graves, Cornwallis left his wounded behind and pressed on.

Today, Guilford Courthouse National Military Park owns only about one-fifth of the land. The rest of the battlefield, mass graves and all, is covered with various apartment complexes such as Battle Forest, Lincoln Green, and Grenadier Guard apartments. The private residences near the park are built over the area of the first line of battle.

Chapter Twelve

With all of this pain and suffering and misery, it should come as no surprise at all that there have been numerous reports of ghostly sightings at Guilford Courthouse National Military Park. Park Historian John Durham told me nearly a dozen of them. Although he has never seen a ghost or experienced anything odd, he is not surprised. He suspects that if there are ghosts haunting the military park, they would know to keep clear of him as he would want to ask them questions about the battle.

One of the more remarkable features of the reported ghosts of Guilford Courthouse National Military Park is their tangibility. Many people have apparently encountered and even interacted with the ghosts and never even knew it was happening at the time.

For instance, throughout the 1960s and 1970s, neighbors in the nearby apartments and residential communities, particularly those in the Battle Forest area, would often call the park and complain about all the noise the horses were making at night. They would ask that something be done to keep the animals quiet. Especially loud were the riders galloping their mounts all throughout the night. Guilford Courthouse National Military Park does not now nor has it ever had stables. Horses were never kept on the property. There could not have been riders racing through the park, and no hoof prints or other signs of evidence have ever been found to substantiate neighbor complaints. It's been about thirty years since anyone has called to complain about horses whinnying nervously in the night, but that doesn't mean that we have heard the last of them.

Every March 15th several reenactment groups come to the park and, within the boundaries available to them, they do what they can to reenact the battle for those who come to watch. On one such occasion one of these actors saw a group of people some distance away. They were interacting with one another socially, but he was sure they were not part of the event. He said it was like they were in a cloud of mist; they were hazy and somewhat fuzzy and eventually...the foggy scene *faded* away.

Back in 2006 an even more interesting and unexplainable encounter happened. Guilford Courthouse National Military Park is a favorite for those who live in Greensboro and enjoy the healthy habit of walking

Guilford Courthouse National Military Park

for exercise, but one of the regular walkers had quite a tale to tell when he returned to the museum.

"John Walker," as I shall call him, walked the park every day. As a matter of habit, he stops at location six, the site of the old courthouse, where there are restrooms and a bench for relaxing. The old courthouse was right in the middle of what we call the third line, where the most intense and the bloodiest part of the battle was fought. Also, it's where some of the park's mass graves are located. Some of these graves are right under the paved walkway itself.

While John Walker sat there resting, a man wearing the uniform of a Continental soldier approached him. Walker later said that he remembered thinking to himself that this guy must be some sort of serious re-enactor as every detail of his uniform was present and expertly crafted as far as he could tell. As a frequent visitor to the park, he had seen the museum's display of uniforms that are there behind glass on many occasions. "Hello. Good day for a reenactment," Walker said. The man looked at him, but made no reply. "Are there many visitors up front?" Walker was curious because he didn't remember there being a battle scheduled for that day, and he didn't recall a bulletin posted on the community board outside the museum's main door listing a time for a skirmish either. He wondered what sort of turnout the actors were going to have with no advertising. How would the community know to show up and watch? The soldier continued not to answer him, and a long and awkward silence passed between the two men. Walker decided to leave; the man was obviously so into his character that he was not going to speak, and he himself needed to finish up his daily constitutional. Walker took a cursory glance back after a few steps and saw that the man was gone already. He gave it no more consideration and finished his daily rounds.

After his walk was over, just as he was about to leave the park, Walker decided to ask about the skirmish, thinking that maybe he would stay and watch it. Inside the museum he was a well-known and familiar face. He asked at the information desk who the soldier was at the third line and when was the battle scheduled for that day. Park staff told him that there were no re-enactors on the site and that there were no activities planned for that day either. John Walker became visibly

Chapter Twelve

shaken and very nervously told his tale of what had just happened to him out on the third line.

Most chilling of all of these stories happened to a woman re-enactor who understandably chooses to remain unnamed. All armies have a cast of support characters who although they do not venture into the line of fire, serve an equally important service. These support personnel stay behind and care for the camp's needs, cooking, tending to the wounded, servicing equipment, and a host of other duties. "Mary Camp" was one of these unsung heroines.

One March 15th the re-enactors were at the park in full force. Costumed players of both sides and every rank were present. After a morning of preparation, the re-enactors finally took their places and began the Battle of Guilford Courthouse yet again. The men went off to war and the women, Mary among them, stayed behind in camp.

As Mary busied herself with her duties, a British soldier came walking into her encampment, saw the fire, and sat down next to it. Had this been a real war I imagine that the camp's response would have been quite different, but Mary saw the man sitting there, alone, and went and sat next to him. They talked for quite a while. It is said that he gave basically yes or no answers to her questions, but didn't contribute otherwise to the conversation. After a while Mary offered the soldier some tea to which he graciously accepted with a sad smile. Mary left to get her tea from her tea chest, but as she turned her back to him, she experienced a most disturbing feeling, like fire and ice racing down her spine. Quickly she turned back around, that awful feeling increasing, but the soldier was no longer there.

When the men came back into camp after the event, Mary described the man and the uniform he wore, wondering who he was, how he got into camp, and where he had gotten off. The actors told Mary that there were no British soldiers on this side of the park. They went on to say that although the person she described did not sound familiar, the uniform did. They showed her pictures from various books to confirm it, but the uniform she described was from the British 33rd, General Cornwallis's own regiment.

Mary still does reenactments, but she has not returned to Guilford Courthouse.

Guilford Courthouse National Military Park

There are other tales of ghostly encounters, and not all of them are as terrifying. Another regular park walker claimed to smell gunpowder as she passed through the third line area. Immediately after, she was struck with a feeling of extreme unease and she shook with the chills.

There have also been reports of the sounds of bagpipes coming from that area. It should be noted that the Highlanders 71st regiment aligned with the British did fight on the field that day.

There are a few buildings in the park, and not surprisingly, they too have had ghostly encounters reported inside of them as well. Quarters Two, as it is called, has caused many of its occupants to lose a night's sleep due to the sounds of footsteps, voices, and other unidentified noises being heard. It's located on the western side of the park.

Quarters Two had been the chief ranger's residence when one resided on the grounds. One of the chief rangers refused to live in the building and opted for commuting to work because of all the odd happenings she encountered.

Another chief ranger who did reside in Quarters Two probably wished he had not. He admitted to hearing noises and footsteps. In fact, one night he woke up because he heard footsteps clearly right outside his bedroom door. When he went to investigate, the footfalls moved down the hall and into another room. The ranger followed as stealthily as he could, but the other person was always just around a corner, out of sight. The footfalls were so clear and distinct that the ranger firmly believed there was a person in the house trying desperately not to be caught. This went on all night long—with him chasing someone he could never quite catch up to.

Also in the military park are the Superintendent's Quarters, located across New Garden Street, opposite from the visitor's center. One of the superintendents who lived in the house believed his residence was haunted. His wife was constantly finding tools moved from one location to another in the basement. Hammers, nails, and screwdrivers would be seen one moment in their proper place on the workbench, and then a moment later they would be over on the other side of the room on a shelf. Definitely a curious happening, but the last superintendent to ever occupy the house had no trouble with haunting-related events of any kind. The house that is still standing on the grounds remains unoccupied to this day.

Chapter Twelve

Park Historian John Durham has heard a number of ghost tales in his more than thirty years of employment at the park, but this one comes from a fellow employee he worked with for many years we'll call for the sake of storytelling "Eve Painter." Her story revolves around the dominating portrait of General Nathanael Greene that hangs in the lobby of the visitor's center.

Like many portrait paintings of its day, the background is very dark, if not altogether black. The clothing of the person is represented in adequate detail, but since it's not the focus of the painting, it too is in vignette. The general's face, serious and determined looking, is just shy of being off-centered and is notably pale in contrast to the rest of the painting. It's not at all how we would commission a painting of ourselves these days, but when the portrait was done, it was the fashion of the time.

Ms. Eve Painter had decided to come back to the museum one evening to finish up some necessary work. Because it was late and the park was closed for the day, she decided to take her dog "Inky" along with her.

After a few hours of work, Painter began to get an uneasy feeling about her. Concerned, she began to walk through the building, her dog following at her heels.

As she walked near the main desk approaching the portrait of General Greene, her dog began to growl and locked eyes with the picture. Painter asked her dog what was wrong, but Inky only continued to stare down the portrait and growl. The feeling of uneasiness that she had experienced earlier had been increasing ever since. A believer in following your gut instincts, she and Inky immediately left the building.

Painter was shaken by the experience, but did not let it interfere with her job. She continued to work at the museum until her retirement, but never again alone, and especially not at night.

Another employee of Guilford Courthouse National Military Park has had more than a ghostly experience, but that's because maybe **he's** the ghost.

One of the long-time employees, "Theodore Samos," as we shall call him, had the habit of wearing his keys on a chain on his belt, and as he walked, the keys would jingle. It was a very distinctive

Guilford Courthouse National Military Park

A typically styled portrait painting of its day, General Nathanael Greene's hangs on the wall in the visitor's center near the Information Desk. Much is known about the man and his military record, but based on one ghostly encounter, one wonders what his opinion of dogs might have been.

sound, unmistakable as to what it was, and at the time only he and Durham wore their keys in that fashion. Samos eventually retired and in due course passed away, but soon after his death, his old friends from work began to hear the familiar jingle of keys. Eve Painter, who had already had her run-in with the portrait of General Greene, also

Chapter Twelve

heard the keys. This did not frighten her, though; as she said, she knew Samos and knew that he would never hurt her or anyone else for that matter.

Finally, one of the oldest stories collected from Guilford Courthouse National Military Park dates from 1888. It has been handed down over the years as originating from local resident Miss Coffin. (Her actual name, I did not make it up!)

Miss Coffin claims that on the northern side of the battlefield the bodies of two British cavalrymen, or *light horses* as they were called at that time, were found. They were memorable among all the other dead found because they had the misfortune to have passed from this world near a freshly uprooted tree. Perhaps it was an opportunity seized, not to have to dig one more grave, but whatever the reason was, the hole the roots of the tree left was used. The soldiers' bodies were rolled into the makeshift grave, the trunk of the tree chopped off, and the newly made stump turned over, burying them. Years later, a road was constructed that ran right past the burial site, and no sooner was it completed than reports that the road was haunted began to spread. Two British cavalrymen could be seen riding white horses down the road, consequently keeping the road clear of traffic at night.

Proof of the belief of this story can be found in a letter written by J. H. Foster to Joseph M. Morehead, dated March 19, 1894: "...for years I dreaded to cross the old battlefield for the...people had filled me with hobgoblins and had seen some of the Light Horse, as they called cavalry then, riding pell-mell without any head and seeing the lights of the trenches where the soldiers were buried."

††††††††††††††

The Guilford Courthouse National Military Park is open to the public year-round from 8:30 a.m. to 5:30 p.m. It is closed only on New Year's Day, Thanksgiving Day, Christmas Eve, and Christmas Day. The visitor's center where the museum is located is free of charge, although donations are always welcome. For further information, please visit the Web site at www.gov/guco or call 336-288-1776.

††††††††††††††

13

Lydia's Bridge

Southern Railroad Underpass Bridge

> "What greater pain could mortals have than this:
> To see their children dead before their eyes?"
> -- *Euripedes (480 BC–406 BC)*

She is by far one of the area's best known and most beloved residents, even though she died going on one hundred years ago, and, technically, died in the suburb community of Jamestown. But the haunting is just over the border and so well known that there cannot be a collection of haunted Greensboro sites and not mention this one. She is known by many names—The Phantom Hitchhiker; The Vanishing Lady; The Lady in White; The Lovely Apparition; The Vanishing Hitchhiker—but the folks around here just call her Lydia. There are varying levels of details that go along with her sad story, but I will give you the most complete telling of the story I have pieced together through the innumerous and various sources available on her and this subject.

One foggy night back in the early 1920s, a beautiful young girl named Lydia was at a dance, some say specifically a prom. She had promised her mother that she would be home by her curfew, but lost track of time at the party as young girls often do. She found her date

Chapter Thirteen

and together they hurriedly left the party, racing for her home. It was very important to the young couple that they make it there before Lydia's curfew. Unfortunately, the young man was not driving as carefully as he could have, and through a combination of haste and the rising thick fog, he lost control of his vehicle on the twisting hilly roads of the area. They crashed head-on into the Southern Railroad Underpass Bridge at high speed. The young and handsome driver of the car died instantly upon impact, but poor Lydia did not. She somehow managed to crawl out of the wreckage, but before she could successfully flag down a passing car for help, she succumbed to her wounds. Passing drivers had obviously mistaken her for a hitchhiker. The community at large was devastated over the senseless and particularly tragic death of two of their own promising young adults. Lydia's mother, a widow already, lost her only child. The boy's family was rather well off and had some degree of local power and influence. It was because of their dogged determination and newspaper coverage that the "old bridge" was closed and a new railroad bridge was built on a section of road that was made straighter and then was newly repaved.

Lydia's Bridge

Now, fast-forward some years later. It is, as the great Victorian novelist Edward Earl Bulwer would say, "a dark and stormy night." A man driving home late in the evening sees just up ahead a young girl in a white dress. He pulls over and offers her a ride home. She accepts his offer and says scant little else as they drive off, no matter how many questions the gentleman driver asks of her. All the girl is really clear about is that she is on her way home and doesn't want her mother to

This is the old bridge, Lydia's Bridge, as seen when coming around the hill, that the power station now rests upon. When this picture was taken, it was what passes for winter here in North Carolina. The mass of greenery around the entrance to the tunnel is kudzu. In the summer, when it is growing three inches a day, the old bridge is completely hidden by a leafy veil.

Chapter Thirteen

worry. Ahead is a small house with a porch light on and the girl motions for the driver to stop there. The driver turns to face his lovely and forlorn companion, but sees that she has disappeared from his car. There is an urge now for the driver to brave the elements, go up the walk, and knock on the little house's door despite the late hour. He manages to convince himself that he wants to do so, to make sure the girl who somehow slipped him got into her home safely. An elderly woman, who looks sad and expectant, almost knowing, answers the door. The man explains he was trying to drop off a young lady who claimed to live here, but that he didn't see her leave his car and just wants to make sure that she got into the house all right. Sadly, the old woman shakes her head. "That was my daughter, Lydia," the old woman would say. "She was killed in a car accident some years ago. You're not the first person who has tried to get her home to me."

Common variations to the story are slight. The year was 1923, not 1924; it was January, it was mid spring; it was cold and raining, it was dark and foggy; it was a New Year's Eve ball, it was a prom; she was waving her arms frantically, she was simply just walking; she was in a white gown covered in blood, she was in a beautiful fancy dress; the driver who picked her up was alone, the driver had a friend with him; she needed a ride to High Point, she needed a ride home; she vanishes out of the car just as they pull up to the house, she vanishes out of the car when the driver goes around outside to open the car door for her; the mother is angry another man tried and failed to deliver her daughter, the mother is sad but compassionate to the man who failed to bring her daughter back home. All slight differences, but nothing so critical. Mix and match them as you, like but the essence of the tale remains the same.

If a master storyteller, such as Greensboro's very own Cynthia Moore Brown, tells Lydia's story, you'd have goose pimples all over your arms and no doubt be inclined to either steer clear of that area at night, or cruise around looking for the ghost. Either way, she'll inspire you.

My assistant Joy and I headed out of Greensboro down High Point Road in the middle of the day in search of Lydia and her bridge. We chose broad daylight not because we were concerned about picking up a phantom hitchhiker, but rather we didn't want to happen upon

Lydia's Bridge

anyone who may be using the old tunnel underpass for any number of nefarious reasons.

Since there is absolutely nowhere to park on the main road without running the risk of becoming the next round of ghosts to have their origins at the bridge, we had to pull into a small housing community and park on the street there. There is a parking lot, but we didn't use it; it could have been restricted to residents only, their vehicle tags with a parking decal or some other means of identification. There weren't any signs warning of such, nor did I see any commonality of a sticker, but I didn't want to risk getting a ticket, let alone getting my car towed. I especially

This is what we call the new bridge, the one where Lydia did not meet her demise. This railroad underpass goes over High Point Road. If you plan on going into Jamestown to see Mendenhall Plantation or Copper Creek, you'll have to pass underneath it.

Chapter Thirteen

did not want to be accused of trespassing on anyone's property; that fine would be more expensive than a ticket and tow combined.

As soon as you announce that you're off to visit Lydia's Bridge, every local will immediately warn you not to be fooled about which bridge on High Point Road is hers. The *real* bridge is off to the side, about two hundred feet further away from the road. I had been told that the original overpass was now opposite a power station, and since something like that is a huge landmark we were able to see it right away. The power station sits atop a hill, and it's the only power station in sight. The "old bridge," Lydia's Bridge, is right on the other side of that hill. I warn you not to be tempted into taking the neat and well-maintained white gravel path around the hill. That would be a clear case of trespassing and there are signs up clearly posting that if you use that path, you'd be breaking the law. Not to mention, the day Joy and I went, there were lots of folks milling about the community. If you must check out the real bridge for yourself, I highly recommend doing so legally by walking all the way around the hill, along the city's grass until it turns into the city's kudzu, and then follow it. The city has not posted any signs warning against trespassing. Eventually you will come across a well-worn deer path or three that are cut into the sea of kudzu. Each one of these paths goes to the tunnel, but depending on your personal level of athleticism, choose the one you feel most comfortable with.

If you decide to go in the winter months like we did to avoid the snakes and rats that may be living in the kudzu, you will have no trouble whatsoever seeing the underpass. It loomed at us like the great gaping hole that it is. However, if you go when the kudzu is lush and alive and growing about three inches a day, it looks like you're going to walk right up to an impenetrable wall of green. Unless you move the hanging greenery aside, you run the risk of walking straight into a wall.

Inside the tunnel every square reachable inch is covered in layers and layers of graffiti. Those who are easily offended need not enter. The tunnel can't be more than fifty feet in length, but it is dark and your voice will make just the slightest echo. It's cooler inside the tunnel too, but I suspect not because it is haunted but rather because it's a cement hole in a hill and such places are always cool. The floor of the tunnel is covered with cigarette butts, broken glass, and other signs of misuse, but underneath all of that debris is a layer of grass. Using

Lydia's Bridge

My assistant and I took many pictures on our trip to Lydia's Bridge in the hopes of capturing something on film. We did not get any ghostly images, no phantom smoke, not even so much as an orb. But this bit of graffiti, about the only nonoffensive writing there, was too funny not to take a picture of. Unless, of course, he really can...

Chapter Thirteen

the heel of my boot, I scraped away a small section of turf and not even an inch down there was road pavement staring up at me. It was a little frightening to see the road and wonder if Lydia walked this way when she tried to look for help. Was I standing where she did? Was this where she died? My assistant took numerous photos in the hopes of capturing a ghostly image or at the very least some orbs we could later speculate about. Unfortunately, we captured neither, but at least one visitor had a sense of humor.

With the site visited and pictures taken, it was time to get to work. Some serious research needed to be done. Who was this young lady who haunts the road, how did she die, what is it that keeps her bound to this world, and why has her story persisted for so long?

Stories of "phantom hitchhikers" have existed for a very long time. Even the ancient Romans had a similarly styled tale. In 1602 Swedish author Petri Klint published *On the Signs and Wonders Preceding the Liturgic Broil* where he told his story of a hitchhiking ghost. There is an English ballad recorded in a 1723 anthology titled *Relation of a Young Man, who, a month after his death, appeared to his Sweetheart, and carried her on horseback behind him for forty miles in two hours, and was never seen after but in his grave.* (A long title to be certain and it pretty much also explains the whole song as well.) Washington Irving's 1824 novel *The Lady With the Velvet Collar* was about a hitchhiker ghost, as was Orson Wells' 1951 film short *Return to Glennascaul*.

Numerous countries from all around the world experienced what can only be described as a rash of phantom and prophetic hitchhikers during the 1970s. In all of these cases just before the ghost disappeared, it gave a prophecy of some description. Although not every prophecy came to pass that would have been truly newsworthy and remarkable, but one alleged prediction by one of these ghosts was—the eruption of Mount St. Helens.

In fact, most major cities have a comparable type of story if you ask around enough, like in Blue Bell Hill in Kent, England; Interstate 5 in Tacoma, Washington; Route 1 outside of Baltimore, Maryland; Kingsway Tunnel in Merseyside, England; and the N2 in Switzerland at Belchen Tunnel, just to name a few. Even a few of the Hawaiian islands have their own ghostly hitchhiker.

Lydia's Bridge

Most folks immediately brush these tales off as archetypical storytelling, urban legends, or some sort of highway hypnosis.

But the story of Lydia is different from all the other tales in that there are *a lot* of specific details to the events leading up to the car accident, as well as what happened before the first ghostly sighting. Lydia's back-story, the very fact she has one, is so much more complete and well rounded than others of its kind. Even if the story of Lydia were not wholly true, maybe it was loosely based on actual events. Maybe our Lydia is not another unsubstantiated urban myth...maybe *our* Lydia was real.

To begin with, High Point Road, the road that passes directly under "Lydia's Bridge" is technically U.S. 29-70A. It was a humble wagon trail for almost one hundred years. In 1908 it was lined in the MacAdam style of road construction, and later in 1914 it was most likely paved over with a layer of sprayed asphalt. The railroad underpass was originally made of wood, but was eventually modernized and given cement reinforcement and a brick face façade.

The first report of Lydia trying to catch a ride home occurred in the spring of 1924. The name of the man who claimed he tried to get her home to her mother was Burke Hardison. In his telling of the events of that night, he was leaving Raleigh and returning to his home in High Point. It had been raining and there was a thick fog that gave him very limited visibility. As he neared the underpass, he saw a girl waving him down. He stopped and she got in the car, saying she was trying to get to her home in High Point. She had left a dance in Raleigh and was worried that her mother would be up worrying about her. Other than getting an address and her first name out of her, Lydia, Hardison could get no other information. He parked the car at the address she gave him and when he came around to open the door for her, she was gone. He decided to go up to the house where he knocked at the door until a woman answered. She listened very politely to Hardison tell his tale. She then told him that her only daughter, Lydia, was killed in a car accident under the railroad underpass last year, and that he was not the first man who had tried, in vain, to bring her back home.

So, according to the very first publicized story told of Lydia, the accident that killed her would have been in the spring of 1923.

Chapter Thirteen

In virtually all the cases where I found the Lydia story printed, the author claimed that for the sake of those who lived in the house now, the address was omitted. I can understand the decency of doing so, but it would make my research that much harder. If that address could be found, maybe, just maybe, there would be surviving family of both Lydia and her young beau. I had thought about how wonderful it would be to find these descendants. Perhaps they still lived in the area and maybe they'd be willing to talk about the event, give their perspective of the incident and how it affected them. Maybe I could even visit and lay flowers at poor Lydia's grave.

I began this search as I did many, at the Greensboro Main Branch Public Library. There, with the help of reference librarian Helen Snow, I was able to peruse the microfiche of the two newspapers that were covering Greensboro and its surrounding area back in the 1920s: the *Greensboro Daily News* and the *Greensboro Daily Record*. I had figured that since the Lydia back story claims that there was a public outcry over the deaths of two young people that there was bound to be mention of the boy's full name and of Lydia's last. Maybe even that elusive address would be given and the name of the cemetery where their young souls were laid to rest.

My ever-faithful assistant Joy and I had to carefully read through a lot of newspaper pages. Before 1978, there are no indexes for looking up stories. So, we had to read the January and February papers for 1923 and 1924 for each of the papers because in none of the stories is there an exact date. The same had to then be done for March and April of 1923 and 1924. I wanted to make sure that if there was a chance in finding out more about Lydia, I didn't miss it. Obviously, this huge of an undertaking made our task a little bit harder, but we had no idea on the onset just how much, lack of indexing aside.

Apparently, newspaper layout has come a long way, and we modern readers have no idea how truly lucky we are in this respect: We have our paper divided up into sections. Today we are able to flip right to our favorite section. Want to know what's going on in the world, like, for instance, how the war in Iraq is doing? Well, just go straight to the World News section and read all about it. Curious about how the vote went on the zoning board? It would be in the Local news section. What theater group is appearing at the Carolina Theatre—that would be in

Lydia's Bridge

the Entertainment section. Likewise, if you were looking for the obituary of a young girl, it would be in the Obituary section.

But back in the 1920s newspapers were laid out very differently. For starters, modern papers have no more than six columns of text, but back then, it was not unheard of to have up to 10. Naturally, the font, or the size of the words, was much smaller to accommodate the increase in the number of columns. Another difference is how the stories were placed on the page. Today's readers can easily tell where one story starts and another begins because the headlines are in a different size font and the stories are typically separated by very thin lines. Also these stories are run "square," that is to say, that when at all possible a story is placed all in the same area of a page so that in the event text wraps from one column to another, it all stays under the headline of the story. Not so back then. Stories would run wild across a page, sometimes filling up an entire column, other times they were slightly offset in a square in the middle of a page with numerous other stories or advertisements running around it. And one final noticeable difference worth mentioning, although there are numerous others, is that the white space of the paper was used to its utmost. Font sizes, kerning, and leading would shift to cram a story into a small space, and quotes were only set off by quotation marks rather than being a stand-alone paragraph. Today's papers take into account a sort of visual aesthetics and use the whiteness of the paper to not only make it overall visually more pleasing to look at as a whole, but also to further differentiate the area between the stories and ads. This is usually accomplished by making each sentence of the story its own paragraph. In short, being a modern reader and unaccustomed to the Helter Skelter layout used in the past, we had to scan every column very carefully to seek out headlines.

After all of this searching and hunting and pecking through entire months of two different newspapers, we found nothing relating to Lydia. No story of a young couple killed in a tragic car crash. No stories about closing a section of the railroad underpass bridge, straightening out a road, or building another railroad underpass to take the old one's place. Not even a mention of the one-year anniversary of any of the above-mentioned events having taken place. In fact, the only public outcry of any kind was because of an ongoing local scandal—a woman,

Chapter Thirteen

thirty-two years of age, was fighting in court to get a marriage license to marry her 22-year-old fiancé. It was getting more attention than the ongoing Irish Civil War.

Disheartening as it was, we decided to press on. Since nearly all the stories were in agreement that the accident took place sometime in January, except for the Hardison version, we decided to check back a year to 1922 and ahead a year to 1925.

The only automobile accident that we found that occurred in the area that also involved the death of a female happened on December 31, 1923. It took place on Spring Garden Street, and the victim, Lucile Gray Allgood, was seven years old. She was run over by a truck, her chest crushed, and she died in the hospital on January 1, 1924, in Winston-Salem.

She could not be our Lydia; none of the facts matched on any of the points, except for the fact they were both female.

It was considerably time-consuming and monotonous reading through the old newspapers. It could take literally months of checking and still come up with no further relevant information. I thought I could shortcut the process if I went to the Guilford County Department of Births and Deaths and just looked for her death certificate. My thinking was that once I found Lydia's death certificate, I would have the exact day she died and be able to go directly to that day's paper for the story and all the other little facts I so wanted to know. I was fully prepared to sit on a cold floor in a dark basement room and look through thousands of manila three-tab folders searching for anyone named Lydia to see how and when she died. I was quite happy to discover that was not going to be the case.

Happily, everything, all birth and death certificates going back much farther than I needed, had been scanned into a computer for public use. There were ample computer stations set up for anyone to use free of charge, and the program that I needed to make use of was the most user-friendly thing I had ever had the pleasure to utilize. By using their system I was able to search entire decades in just moments. All I had to do was select "Deaths" for the type of certificate I was looking for, enter a range of years into the field provided, and since all I had was a first name, I supplied that bit of information as well.

Lydia's Bridge

In moments, every person who had the word *Lydia* in their name and had died between 1915 and 1935 was at my disposal. There were quite a few, as I discovered that Lydia was something of a popular first and middle name back then. Each scanned document came up to the screen in mere moments, and after I had found where the Cause of Death area was located on the first one, I was able to scan the other documents much more quickly.

There is a person on the Internet who pops up from time to time claiming that he searched through the birth and death certificates as well, and further claims that he found a death certificate for a nineteen-year-old girl who died December 31, 1923. He gives her name as Lydia Jane M—he did not want to give a last name, citing the tried-and-true "for the protection of the family." And if this certificate existed, I would have agreed with him. But I looked, using that name and date. It's not there. In fact, there was not a single Lydia Jane with any last name who died in the twenty-year span we searched.

But I did find this: An automobile struck Lydia J. Fields of Walnut Street on December 8, 1921. She was pronounced dead six hours later.

And that's about all she had in common with the Lydia in our story.

"Housewife" was listed under the heading of Occupation on her Death Certificate, although she was a widow when she died at the age of sixty years, two months, and twenty-eight days.

If you want a copy for yourself, bring a nickel, the cost of an uncertified copy of a Death Certificate. If you want it certified, it costs $10. There is a very brief form you'll need to fill out; it's maybe four or five lines long. The certificate is located in Book Eight, page 768.

Now, does that mean that the ghost of Lydia does not exist, that she is not real? No, in fact, it does not. I was informed by psychic Rowan Wolfe that our Lydia may in fact be there after all, even though she never lived or died. She explained to me that our girl could be a *thought form*.

"Reality is what you believe it to be." It's a Tibetan philosophy and the basic premise of what a thought form, or *tupla,* is. It is believed that if enough sentient beings for a long enough period of time believe something to be true, they unknowingly can give it a form and consciousness of its own. This new being, the thought form, once it's created, is no longer under the control of those who helped forge it,

Chapter Thirteen

This is a copy of the non-certified death certificate for a Mrs. Lydia J. Fields. She is the only Lydia in the entire Piedmont Triad area who died as a result of an automobile accident in the 1920s. Because none of the facts from the Lydia story match the facts regarding the death of Mrs. Fields, she cannot be the same Lydia who haunts the Southern Railroad Underpass Bridge.

but will operate within the parameters that defined its reality set during the creation process.

Ergo, enough people believed the Lydia story and over the years created her ghost. The ghost, now its own person so to speak, is acting out as the story describes. This being said, even someone who is brand-new to Greensboro and has never heard of Lydia, or of any type of phantom hitchhiker story, can still drive down High Point Road until it enters Jamestown, see a girl needing a ride, pick her up, try to drop her off, and fail. Neat.

14

Mendenhall Plantation

> "History is the witness that testifies to the passing of time;
> it illumines reality, vitalizes memory,
> provides guidance in daily life and brings us tidings of antiquity."
> -- *Cicero (106 BC–43 BC)*

Mendenhall Plantation is on the National Register of Historic Places and has been owned by the Historic Jamestown Society since 1985. This three-acre property is basically all that's left of the small Quaker community that resided there. It is, in fact, literally just down the road from Lydia's Bridge (see "Lydia's Bridge" section). There are many outbuildings on the property, including a corncrib, springhouse, and a museum that holds the Ragsdale Arrowhead Collection. The schoolhouse that is on the property was not part of the original plantation, but was moved there in 1985 to save it from demolition and to see to its restoration.

Jamestown is named for James Mendenhall. He was a tanner by trade and left his home state of Pennsylvania during the Revolutionary War to come to North Carolina. Although the exact date is not known, the cornerstone of his house is dated 1765. James's son, Richard, was born during the war. Although he did his apprenticeship in Pennsylvania as a barn builder, when he returned to North Carolina he became a tanner like his father.

Richard went on to found his own home, Mendenhall Plantation. The exact date again is not known, but when the home had additional

Chapter Fourteen

rooms added on, the cornerstones of them were dated 1811. Richard had several children with his wife Mary Pegg; Minerva was their eldest child. She was born inside the family home in 1830. She never married, had no children of her own, and when she died in 1900 inside the very home where she was born, she had outlived her entire family. She was buried in Deep River Meeting Cemetery, and yet some people will have you believe that she still resides in the family home to this day.

Minerva was a very proactive person in life. She focused her attention on the improvement and betterment of this world for the sake of others and was driven by her sense of social activism. She, like many Quaker women, fully embraced the freedom that their religion allowed everyone. Simply put, Quakers believe that every man, woman, and child has an inner light that God speaks to them through. If all people have this light and all people are equal, then it follows that one person cannot own another person because you cannot own the light of God.

Mendenhall Plantation

Picturesque setting atop an embankment, this Bank-style barn was built by Richard Mendenhall. As a child, his apprenticeship was as a barn builder in Pennsylvania.

Minerva would have been against slavery and I imagine that if the question "I'm just one person, what can I do?" were ever put to her, she would have given you fairly precise instructions.

The Mendenhall's Pennsylvanian-style "Bank Barn" was one of the many stops on the Underground Railroad. It was Richard's apprenticeship that no doubt had to do with the design of the barn. In Pennsylvania, the Bank style was common, but here in North Carolina it was altogether unique. Bank style refers to the fact that the barn is intentionally built over a hill, slope, or bank so that the part that would hang off is then built up and used as additional space.

Today the barn houses one of the two original remaining false-bottom wagons that were used to transport slaves to freedom across the border. The only other original wagon still in existence is in the Levi Coffin House and Museum in Fountain City, Indiana.

Chapter Fourteen

Helping transport stolen property across state lines was as much a crime then as it is today. That is exactly the crime that was being committed when people were helping slaves escape to freedom. Interfering with the recovery of an escaped slave was a very serious crime punishable by exceptionally steep fines and imprisonment. Deciding to make your home into one of the "stations" on the Underground Railroad was a radical idea at the time, even for the progressive and proactive set. Fortunately for the Mendenhalls, there is no record of them ever having been caught.

The kitchen in the family home had a hiding place, a small 5-by-12-foot hole in the floor. It is believed that it was used to quickly stash away slaves seeking their freedom until it was safe for them to move on. We can only suspect this is the case because there are no family records mentioning the hole or making reference to one.

On a side note, the Chadwick family, the second owners of the house, eventually upgraded the house with plumbing and electricity.

A piece of history, this is one of the remaining false-bottom wagons actually used to transport slaves to freedom.

Mendenhall Plantation

These upgrades where made throughout, except for in the kitchen. The Chadwicks chose not to make any improvements there. The house was continually lived in as a private residence until 1957 when William Ragsdale purchased it from the Chadwicks in order to preserve it for posterity.

For me, it's hard to imagine that in 1957 there were still people cooking three meals a day by choice over a fire pit, because that is exactly what the Chadwicks were doing. By 1930 most American families had either an electric or gas stove and were in the process of switching over to an electric refrigerator. It was hard for me to wrap my mind around this concept. This was the very period of time that TV shows like *Happy Days* and *Laverne and Shirley* took place in, just a few years before the setting of another popular TV show, *The Wonder Years*. This is the era that my parents grew up in, a time of Elvis and fin-tail cars.

To help emphasize to you how remarkable I find this to be, here is a brief list of other things that were happening in 1957 while the Chadwicks were cooking their meals over an open fire:

- The Frisbee hit toy store shelves
- The Brooklyn Dodgers moved to Los Angeles
- Future astronaut John Glenn flew a supersonic jet from California to New York in just under three and a half hours
- The International Atomic Energy Agency was established
- IBM's 704 computer was being used to track the Russian satellite *Sputnik 1* as it orbited the Earth
- Toyota was beginning to export cars into America
- Americans were being asked by the *Gaither Report* to build their own fall-out shelters
- The Boeing 707 was being used commercially

†††††††††††††††

But, I digress.

Back in the mid-1800s, North Carolina state law dictated that their owners could not free slaves unless "meritorious circumstances" were involved. Then, once freed, the former slave was not allowed to

Chapter Fourteen

stay within the boundaries of the state. Newly free, with no means or income, and an immediate necessity to flee the state without family—these were all frightening prospects. It is said that at this time it was not surprising to hear that a Quaker would step in and lend a hand. Very often, they would then purchase the rest of the former slave's family and cite the "meritorious circumstance" as being "the child of a newly freed parent" and help them all across the border together. I find this to be quite a remarkable act of human kindness and charity.

Minerva was not the sort of person you would think would have become a ghost. She was a teacher, post-mistress, took in and raised orphans, and died a rather peaceful death. There seemed to be no unfinished business or lingering regrets she voiced a need to fulfill on her peaceful deathbed.

And yet, from time to time, folks who visit the plantation claim to see her walking the lawn between the home and the barn. They say she is carrying a basket, which she carefully balances on her hip, as she opens up the large barn door that her father built and slips inside, vanishing before even having the chance to close the door behind her.

†††††††††††††††

Mendenhall Plantation is located at 603 West Main Street and is open to the public Tuesdays through Fridays 11 a.m. to 2 p.m., Saturdays from 1 to 4 p.m., and Sundays from 2 to 4 p.m. It's closed Mondays. Admission is $2 for adults and $1 for children, seniors, and students. For more information visit the Web site www.mendenhallplantation.org or call 336-454-3819.

†††††††††††††††

15

Purgatory Mountain

> "Be gentle with the young."
> -- *Juvenal (1st century, BC)*

Greensboro has for a long time considered itself "the Gateway" to the North Carolina State Zoological Park and Botanical Gardens. Indeed, there are numerous billboards scattered all over the city advertising that very sentiment. Many hotels and restaurants even offer discounts to visitors of the park. Brochures for the zoo are found in many appropriate locations.

The truth being told, the city of Greensboro is a great place for a family to vacation. There are numerous movie theaters; Emerald Pointe Water Park; the Greensboro Children's Museum; The Natural Science Center of Greensboro, home to a petting zoo and planetarium; ArtQuest, a hands-on children's museum; the Ice House Skating Rink; and a Celebration Station, which is an arcade, batting range, go-cart racing, miniature golf course, house o' fun.

What the city cannot offer is the zoo itself, for that is actually located about thirty miles south in the nearby city of Asheboro in Randolph County. It's easy to get to—a straight shot down highway 220/73 South with signs clearly marking the way. Unfortunately for Asheboro, it doesn't really have a wide selection of family-suitable hotels. Additionally, it has until recently been the largest "dry" city in North America, which has caused it to have a truly limited

Chapter Fifteen

variety of dining experiences. There are also no evening nightspots for the adult set to enjoy whatsoever.

But the zoo itself is amazing fun and very child friendly. It is the country's largest walk-through zoo and has been divided up into zones, each one featuring one of the continents. But fear not, there are numerous tram stops and they run frequently. This is a big plus, for the African Plains exhibit, a thirty-seven-acre area, is bigger than many other city's entire zoos. The North American and African exhibits are another five hundred acres, eleven acres of which are dedicated to the zoo's collection of bison and elk.

All the animals are in "as natural as possible" environments. If you just follow the paved walkway, it will take you right past every animal exhibit in the zoo. There are opportunities to take a scenic route to better enjoy the specialty plants and exotic flowers

Purgatory Mountain

that are showcased. On either path there are several rest stops. Water fountains are everywhere, but on the truly hot days look for the "misting points." These are showerheads set up free of charge to instantly refresh your whole being, provided you don't mind a total body wet-down.

With all of this in mind, please note that the zoo is built on Purgatory Mountain, one of the thirty-four mountains in the city of Asheboro and one of the oldest mountains in the world. Time has worn it down to a mere 938 feet above sea level—small for a mountain, but a long up-hill walk when navigating the zoo. Personally, I cannot emphasize or recommend enough how wonderful the zoo's trams are and to use them as often as possible. I promise you will not miss any of the animal attractions, but you will forego some of the botanical arrangements.

All of the child-friendly features of the zoo are big attractions to parents and school groups that frequent the park. But it makes me wonder how many of them know the story of the Legend of Purgatory Mountain?

A lot of people like to refer to the area as being part of the Uwharrie Mountains, and I suppose that's true enough, but not actually the truth. The land grant that was issued gave 1,371 acres of land from *Purgatory Mountain* to be designated and developed into the state's Zoo and Botanical Gardens back in 1971. But you have to admit, building a zoo on a place called Purgatory "anything" sounds pretty creepy.

Many folks will tell you that the mountain got its name back during the Depression era. They say that bootleggers used the mountain. These hardened men would make their stills in secret, hard-to-reach locations so that neither government enforcers nor their own local moonshine competitors could find them. It was said that you could see the eerie yellow lamplights of the rumrunners as they navigated the mountainside at night. These lights were explained to those who questioned them as being ghost lights, lost souls wandering the mountain, ergo the name Purgatory Mountain.

What a great and creepy tale, but it's not wholly true either. There were indeed bootleggers who used the mountain during that time, but that is not how the mountain got its name.

Chapter Fifteen

The name "Purgatory" was being used to describe that particular mountain even back during the Revolutionary War. Further back than that, I can't say who named it, or why.

But the story of the Legend of Purgatory Mountain takes place during the Civil War. Quakers mostly lived in the area back then, and being people who followed a religion of peace as a generality, they did not send their men or young boys off to fight. At the onset of the Civil War, a recruitment station was established in the area, and for three years the officer who worked that post did so with honor, integrity, and dignity, if not much success. He respected the Quakers and did little to pressure them into joining the war, causing him to have uneventful, unremarkable, even dreadful recruitment numbers.

However, near the end of the war, the Confederate army was growing increasingly desperate for able-bodied men to fight for the cause. A new recruiter was sent to Purgatory Mountain, and he was given orders to succeed where his predecessor had failed. He was ordered to recruit men into service by any means. He was not a civil or polite man; in fact, he was described as being flat-out evil. He and his hired cohorts roamed the countryside armed and would literally press men into service. His unethical practices deservedly earned him the nickname of "the Hunter." His most reprehensible and damning act was when he gathered up twenty-two of the local boys. They were all children under the age of thirteen. He had them tied together like pack animals and then forcibly marched in a particularly cold December to a Confederate outpost in Wilmington, a daunting 147 miles.

When the children had reached the eastern side of the state, there was an opportunity for them to make their escape. Taking it, they helped one another on their perilous journey back home. They faced freezing temperatures where they had to huddle together for warmth and shelter, especially during the snowstorms. Extra care had to be taken, slowing them up, as they attempted to cross over the swollen rivers. The water was so cold that if any of them fell in, just a few moments of submersion would kill them. Most of the time there was little or no food, and it was not uncommon for them to go several days without eating. All the while they knew

Purgatory Mountain

that the Hunter had to be close behind, angry and determined to recapture his prey.

It took the children over two months, but they finally made it back home. Knowing that the ruthless Hunter was pursuing them, they fled into the safety of nearby Purgatory Mountain to hide. At night, they would break into small groups and slip back to their families just long enough to receive rations and assure them of their safety. Then they would head back up into the mountain and return to their hiding place. By day the Hunter forced his way into the family's homes, breaking anything or anyone who tried to stop him in his search for the children who had made him look foolish.

About mid-winter the children had realized that the Hunter was not going to leave without them and that his violence upon their families, which was escalating, was going to only get worse and worse. Amongst themselves the three best marksmen came together at Panther Creek and formulated a plan.

One cold winter morning, the three young Quaker boys set themselves up in ambush spots as best they could. Patiently they waited, watching the cabin that the Hunter had claimed as his home. Eventually the man they had feared and dreaded for so long, who had terrorized them and their families, stepped out his front door, gun in hand as he was ready to set out in pursuit of his prey. Shots rang out loud in the cold morning air, finding their mark. The Hunter of Purgatory Mountain was dead before his body hit the cold ground.

To be sure he was dead and not playing possum or was only badly wounded, the boys ran to the body. True enough, two of them had hit their mark, and it was enough to kill him. To prove to the other boys it was safe to come out of hiding and return to their families, the little marksmen cut the brass buttons off the Hunter's Confederate uniform as proof of their success.

All the boys returned home, assuring their families that the Hunter was gone and could bother them no longer. Soon after, the Civil War ended, and life returned to as normal as it could.

But a few years later, sightings of a man wandering the rocky outcrops of the mountain had been reported. He was most often seen in the hours before dawn, his Confederate uniform jacket wide open and unbuttoned.

Chapter Fifteen

Perhaps it was ignored at first; many folks still had and some even still wore their old army uniforms. But the years rolled on, and on, and on. His sightings were always the same, and if this was a real man, it could no longer be the one first spotted all those years ago. The idea that had been whispered at first began to find a voice growing louder and louder as time passed, until someone finally named him when they said, "It must be the Hunter of Purgatory Mountain."

Ironic isn't it, that a ghost who haunts a zoo is called the Hunter? And that he is trapped in limbo in a place called Purgatory Mountain? But isn't it truly frightening that his quarry of choice is not any of the exotic animals located there, but rather little children?

†††††††††††††††

The North Carolina Zoo and Botanical Gardens is open every day except for Christmas Day and days of severe weather. From April 1 to October 31 it is open from 9 a.m. to 5 p.m. From November 1 to March 31 it is open from 9 a.m. to 4 p.m. Adult ticket price is $10, senior citizens and students with a valid ID is $8, while children from 2 years of age to 12 is only $6. Check the Web site www.nczoo.org for additional information, such as a schedule of special events, facilities and amenities offered, and discounted group rates for schools and scout groups. For further information please call 1-800-488-0444.

†††††††††††††††

16

Richfield Road

Gravity Hill

> "You will do foolish things, but do them with enthusiasm."
> -- *Colette (1873-1954)*

All over the world there are reports of mysterious or supernatural places that for lack of a more creative name have been aptly called "gravity hills." In some places they are called a "gravity spot," a "magnetic hill," a "mystery spot," or something along those lines. In fact, I have found that twenty-nine different countries from all over the world have such a location, and they are as similarly named. In the United States, thirty of our fifty states report having them. Some states, like North Carolina, have more than one. We have, as a matter of fact, four. Five if you count Richfield Road.

A "gravity hill," the terminology I prefer, is in fact not as mysterious as it sounds. It's not even really a supernatural location, but rather a proven scientific optical illusion. Usually, in these places, the horizon line is blocked from view, typically by trees. The trees that grow in the area are naturally assumed by the mind to be growing up straight when in fact they are growing at an angle. Therefore, when a gradual slope is encountered, the mind, lacking

Chapter Sixteen

the relevant point of reference a horizon line provides, fills in the blanks, creating an optical illusion. In reality a car, for example, is on a downward slope and is in truth rolling downhill in complete compliance with the law of nature we like to call gravity. It is only our perception of the environment that makes it look like it's rolling uphill. Nevertheless, it's neat to see and very fun to experience, even knowing how the "magic" works.

There are a great number of wild stories circulating on the Internet. One in particular however caught my attention because it was about a paranormal phenomenon that occurs in Greensboro. You would think that when I asked around about it someone would have heard about it. Sadly, this is not the case. Numerous paranormal Web sites say that Richfield Road in Greensboro is our very own gravity hill. If the Web sites can be believed, once on Richfield, pop your car into neutral and wait. The story goes that within moments, the ghost of a woman who apparently died on that road many years ago will come and begin to push your car backward up the hill. No reason for her wanting to do so is given,

Richfield Road

by the way. Even scarier than that, it's also said that if you sprinkle baby powder over the hood of your car before the event happens, when you reach the summit, you'll be able to see her handprints.

From time to time and Web site to Web site, the story varies. In the most modern telling of the tale, the narrator will say that he intended to record the event with a handheld camcorder, but its batteries went dead moments before the car mysteriously started rolling. As is the case with so many tales of urban legends, the narrator of the story, or in these cases, the people making the posts on various Web sites, claim that they were not the person who drove to the spot, and therefore are not able to give directions to the exact location. The narrator of one site I stumbled upon had mentioned that he recalled taking a turn off Summit Avenue and another turn off Battlefield. Beyond that, all he remembered is that Richfield turned into an on ramp to an unnamed highway that headed toward Madison.

Naturally, none of the sites that talk about this phenomena happening here in Greensboro give what I would consider at best even loose directions. Fortunately for us we live in a world where personal, handheld navigational devices exist. I happen to own one such GPS device and was able to navigate to Richfield Road with my assistant Joy riding shotgun. We arrived there with startling ease.

We were both rather surprised when we actually turned onto Battlefield Road. We did not expect any of the postings' information to be accurate. From Battlefield, we turned onto New Garden Road, and from that onto Richfield Road. We knew that this area of Greensboro was ripe with ghost stories because of Guilford Courthouse National Military Park being so close (see section of same name). So there was some initial speculation that perhaps there was some truth to the story.

Richfield Road is indeed a road with a slight incline; some folks would even go so far as to say it has many hill-like qualities for a residential urban area. What it clearly is not is an on-ramp to any highway, but rather a dead-end road. In fact the street sign for Richfield Road is even marked with the words "Street Ends" on it.

Chapter Sixteen

At both the wide base of Richfield Road and the top of the hill with an area big enough to easily make a U-turn in, the ground is fairly level. I know this because I had the foresight to take a level with me. I sprinkled both the hood and the trunk of my car with baby powder even though it was already covered with the bright green pollen that is typical of a North Carolina spring. Then, as per the instructions, at the bottom of the hill, I popped the car into neutral and waited for the ghost of an unnamed lady who had died an unspecified number of years ago from unknown causes to come and for no real reason, begin to push my car up a hill, a la Sisyphus. And waited. And then gave it just five more minutes before deciding that I had wasted enough gas from my car as I sat there with the engine idling.

I was really disappointed that nothing happened; I had truly wanted this to work. I wanted to live near a gravity hill that I could show off to my family and friends. I figured that since we were already there and had already sprinkled the baby powder on my car that we may as well try a few different spots at the base of the road, and from each direction. This was easy enough to accomplish since dead-end roads, even in Greensboro, are not so often used.

If the poor ghost of a woman did indeed show up, she did not put her hands in the baby powder I was now going to have to wash off my car. If she tried with all her might to push my little Kia Sophia with her shoulder, she had no success with that either. In fact, she did not even have the non-corporeal energy to drain the battery from my MP3 player that I listened to while waiting for the car to begin to mysteriously roll of its own accord while simultaneously blocking out Joy's laughter at nothing happening.

Before we left, I felt it my duty to at least make sure gravity was still working in the area. From the top of Richfield Road I drove my car off the level area and nearer to what I supposed would be the *top* of the hill. There I placed my car in neutral and took my foot off the brake. The Kia rolled downhill just fine. At the bottom, after having safely stopped, I did get out and check the trunk of my car to see if the ghostly lady at least gave us a good push to get us rolling. Sadly, there were still no handprints on my car and I would in fact have to hit a drive-through car wash before heading home for the day.

Richfield Road

Clearly marked on the road sign as being a dead end, Richfield Road has a reputation on the Internet as being a gravity hill. The reality is harsh, but we had a good time entertaining the few people who watched us first sprinkle my car with baby powder and then sit on the bottom of the hill waiting for the ghost to play her part. We all got a good laugh out of it, except for Lady Sisyphus who sadly did not show.

I have to admit that I really wanted Richfield Road to be one of these world-renowned gravity hills. I wanted to experience for myself the excitement of seemingly rolling uphill as if propelled by some supernatural force. Fortunately, as I have stated earlier, there are four such locations in North Carolina where I can go and do just that. Richfield Road is just not one of them.

17

Salon Blu'

> "If you love me as I love you, no knife shall cut our love in two."
> -- *Popular nursery rhyme*

On the corner of South Elm and Washington Streets sits the Vernon Building. Two stories tall, made of brick, and using the Italianate Revival style with metal fretwork window lintels, it was built during the Victorian era by the Vanstory Clothing Company in either 1883 or 1890, sources conflict. Either way you like it, it's one of the older buildings still being used downtown.

Back then, shoppers from all over the Piedmont came to downtown Greensboro via electric streetcars, seeking quality clothing of good design in the height of fashion. Vanstory Clothing was competing against the Belk Brothers Company and Sears, Roebuck and Company, both of which were just a few storefronts away on either side. Schiffman's Jewelry was also one of the shops establishing themselves on South Elm Street back then. It opened its doors in 1893 and they, too, are still open to this very day.

According to an article I found in the *Greensboro News and Record,* the Vernon Building was named after a Mrs. Virginia Vernon, who was the owner of record back in 1887, and not her husband, Richard. She renamed the building and had the new name placed on a top cornice, and it can still be found there today. When she died, the building was left as part of an inheritance to her two bachelor sons.

Salon Blu'

The building was eventually renovated and divided up over the years. Storefronts were built for the downstairs and the open top floor was worked into a number of apartment homes. I spoke to one of the current tenants, "Rebecca," who not only lives in the upstairs apartment, but she works in Salon Blu' located directly downstairs.

Rebecca used to work out on the East Coast in a day spa as a masseuse and facial therapist. As she worked, she would on occasion see a woman striding purposefully down the hall, her long blond hair bouncing as she went. Rebecca never thought to mention it to anyone; it was a spa after all, with many repeat

Chapter Seventeen

customers. It would not have been so unusual to see a beautiful woman walking down the hall as if late to an appointment. There was no reason to suspect that she was anything else, or even the same person every time, until it came up in casual conversation among the staff. "Have you seen the ghost yet, a blond-headed woman who rushes down the halls?"

Rebecca has had another experience out West as well. Her boyfriend, Mike, had fallen gravely ill and the prognosis was not favorable. However, before he passed on, Mike managed to promise that he would somehow come back just long enough to let her know that he was all right and at peace.

One day after his passing, Rebecca, at home and alone, felt a need to walk across the room and stand behind one of her chairs. As a masseuse, her hands are her trade. She reached out and believes she felt her beloved Mike's face in her hands. As she caressed the all-too-familiar contours, she was suddenly reassured that he was keeping the promise he had made to her. Mike was there, just like he promised her he would be. She was instantly assured that he did not want her to be sad, he was at peace.

So, after moving across the country to start a new job and live in a new apartment, she finds herself yet again surrounded by ghosts.

Salon Blu' is a very modern and swank hair salon situated inside the Vernon Building. It's easy to forget once you are inside that you are in downtown Greensboro and not at some world-famous Paris salon.

I heard the story of the ghosts from a few different people, and although I was not able to historically verify it, it's nevertheless not only possible, but also a fitting dish of gossip for a hair salon.

Once upon a time, back when the Vernon Building was wholly devoted to the textile industry, an unnamed husband and wife operated it. Among the many staff they employed was one young girl of particular note, also unnamed. She was special because the husband and she were in love with one another. There is no evidence in the story as to say whether they ever consummated their love for one another. On the other hand, the story claims that the wife was the devil herself to work for and that she was particularly mean

Salon Blu'

to the ladies of the staff. Hunting was not an uncommon sport for gentlemen to enjoy, and apparently this was one of the husband's passions. The wife arranged a safari for her husband, dutifully making all the arrangements herself. Among the people she hired to accompany her husband was an assassin whose duty it was to arrange an "accidental" shooting. The wife's plan went off without a hitch, and if she was ever implicated (which I personally doubt considering the mindset of the capabilities of women during that era), it was never mentioned in any of the versions of the story I was told. The young girl was inconsolable over the tragic death of her beloved, and as is many times the case, she soon succumbed to her sadness and died of a broken heart. Normally this would be the end of such a tale, but this being a ghost story, it is not the case. The two would-be lovers are now united in death as ghosts, together forever, haunting the Vernon Building, happily ever after. Or so the story ends.

Rebecca knew that there was at least one ghost in the building before she even heard the story of the jealous wife, adulterous husband, and forlorn shop keep girl. She told me that one day while sitting at the front counter, she kept hearing a thumping sound. Whenever she would turn to see what could be causing it, the noise would stop. It happened on and off, and just when she had about convinced herself that it wasn't really anything or even in their part of the building, she heard footsteps right behind her.

There *she* was, a small woman hunched over a bundle of fabrics. She was folding or sorting them very quickly. Her dress was long and covered with an apron; there was a "Gibson Girl" quality about her. And then...*she* was gone. For just a moment she was there hard at work; the next, nothing but a memory.

Because Rebecca already had some experience with the supernatural, she was not too badly shaken up. She told her coworkers what she had seen, and they confided to her the story of the mistress who died of a broken heart.

That night, after the salon was closed and Rebecca retired to her apartment above, she decided she needed to have a talk with the spirit she had seen earlier that day. She told me that she spoke aloud saying, "I live and work here now. I don't mean you

Chapter Seventeen

any harm. I'm a single girl like you and I lost someone that I love too. Let's be friends."

Rebecca said that from time to time she will hear heavy footfalls, a man's, walking through her apartment, but she doesn't let it bother her. She's never felt afraid in her home, nor has she ever experienced anything bad in either the salon or her home. She believes that it's most likely the husband en route to meet his beloved shop keep girl.

✝✝✝✝✝✝✝✝✝✝✝✝

Salon Blu' is a five-star reviewed hair, nail, and beauty salon located in the Vernon Building on South Elm Street.

✝✝✝✝✝✝✝✝✝✝✝✝

18

Twin Lakes Lodge

> "The soul of man is immortal and imperishable."
> -- *Plato (427 BC–347 BC)*

You would never know that amidst the hustle and bustle of Four Seasons Town Centre and High Point Road that there is a small eight-acre lake surrounded by a forest of hickory and dogwood trees. All around this lake are beautiful and secluded homes. One of these homes has been turned into a luxurious bed-and-breakfast and is now known as the Twin Lakes Lodge. Aside from rooms in the main house, there is also the Cottage, home to the Tree House suite and the Lake View Landing suite. Among the many fine features of this bed-and-breakfast are the king-size beds; fireplaces; whirlpools; in-house masseuse, facial and body wrap expert; and private limousine services. It's a perfect place to stay if you're honeymooning or just looking for a romantic weekend away from it all with that special someone.

Twin Lakes Lodge, owned and operated by Anita Gill, is actually two houses on the same property and has something of a noteworthy history all to itself. The land was marched over by General Cornwallis's men on their way to the Battle of Guilford County Courthouse to lock horns with General Greene (see section "Guilford Courthouse National Military Park"). The main house was the home of John Harden, author of *Tar Heel Ghosts* and *The Devil's Tramping Ground and Other North Carolina Mystery Stories*. His

Chapter Eighteen

son, John Harden, Jr., said that his father built the house in 1963 and lived there till his death in 1985.

All in all, it is a beautiful and restful spot, and if one were resigned to having to spend eternity haunting a place, they could do a lot worse than Twin Lakes Lodge.

The lake near the lodge is similar to many other lakes scattered throughout the state. And unfortunately like too many of them, it has been the location of the loss of life connected to an accident. It's been said that back in the 1960s, a child drowned out there on the lake. Too sad to be true, but yet his little spirit, if not at eternal rest, is not wholly unhappy either. On the rare occasion a guest of

Twin Lakes Lodge

This lovely view was taken from the front steps of Twin Lakes Lodge. It is so peaceful and serene here that you would never know how close you are to Four Seasons Town Centre, the coliseum, and the downtown area. The sounds of cars and sirens cannot penetrate into this little patch of woods.

the lodge, while bragging to Anita about how peaceful and tranquil the house is, will make mention that even the child they saw playing outside was quiet and respectful of the property. Anita knows that there are no children in the neighborhood, and she would certainly be aware if a guest checked in with one. However, over the years the description of the child is basically the same, making her wonder if it's a ghost or not.

Some time ago, three well-known paranormal investigators and a psychic led by paranormal radio talk show host J. Scott visited the Twin Lakes Lodge to see what, if anything, they could turn up. I spoke with J. about his investigation there, and what follows is what he told me happened that night.

The basement of the house, like many basements, is a cool, creepy, and perfect place to set up some listening devices. The

Chapter Eighteen

Not a part of the house used by visitors, we were given special permission to take a look at the basement. This is where paranormal investigators have in the past set up sound recording devices in an attempt to capture ghostly voices.

goal was to see if any electronic voice phenomena, or EVP, could be picked up and recorded. Some people believe that an EVP is the voice of a ghost, while others dismiss it as static, background noise, or any other number of excuses. Other places in the house were set up with similar equipment.

Video cameras were put in place to record the evening event, and laptop computers were used to coordinate activities. The event was to be broadcast live for J.'s radio show and podcast, "The World of Darkness." The psychic who was present planned a séance for that evening as well.

J. told me that from the beginning of their investigation they were set upon by paranormal activity. Orbs were showing up in their photography; the air conditioner unit was turning itself on and off, as was the ceiling fan, VCR, and clock radio. Messages were being typed out on the laptop by unseen hands. Also, while they were on-air that night, the fader board buttons on the soundboard moved all by themselves. Most frightening, I find, is that the electric clocks in

Twin Lakes Lodge

the room all blinked off at midnight, while no other electric devices suffered a power failure or brownout. Meanwhile, an alarm clock in a back room rang out loudly.

When later examined, the EVP equipment picked up what the investigators believed to be the sound of a man's voice. Another of the EVP microphones picked up what can only be described as the sound of a washing machine, which would be normal and expected if there was one in the room for it to record.

The psychic claimed that she was hearing someone humming and occasionally calling out her name. She said that she was picking up on a strong female presence in the room that was looking after someone, but was unable to make any further contact with it.

While I was there, Anita showed me pictures of a red, yellow, and gold prismatic ghost fire, or "flame," for lack of a better word, that was taken in one of the rooms by one of the paranormal investigators. When asked if there had ever been a fire in the history of the house, she said yes but "not a bad one." In the attic, suspiciously right over the spot where the "flame bow" picture was

A view of the living room. All the areas of the house are beautifully decorated and have a wonderfully homey feel to them.

Chapter Eighteen

taken, there is a small bit of scorch mark on some of the rafters. Anita had always speculated that perhaps it was a very small fire, the type that is started by someone trying to sneak a cigarette. It was not so bad that it warranted replacing or even restoring the beams. Additionally, she added, no one had ever been seriously hurt in the house, let alone died there. Which made me wonder, if there was no tragic fire, why was there a "ghost fire" present?

In all of my wanderings and research for this book, I had never once set out with the idea of "busting" a myth or proving or disproving a ghost story. My sole intent had always been to record the history of a place, including any ghost tales or legends of a haunting that may be attached. We can't pick and choose our history; it all belongs to us—the good, the bad, and the unexplained. But I feel that this next little story is relevant and worth mentioning, since I was there at Twin Lakes Lodge with my assistant Joy and photographer Karl Farago when it happened.

I was checking out the bathroom where the EVP picked up the washing machine sounds when I heard the two of them giggling with

This is the area of the house where the "flamebow" was taken. Although we had taken numerous pictures of the phenomenon when it occurred on our visit, none of them reproduced well enough to show here.

Twin Lakes Lodge

the sound of excitement that is attached to discovery. Immediately upon my entering the room, Farago showed me an image he had captured on his digital camera—it was our very own flame bow. Shocked and amazed, I stared at the digital image until he told me to look up. There, *floating* not five feet away from us was...a red, yellow, and golden prism.

Fortunately, before I had the opportunity to go into cardiac arrest from a combination of elation and fear, we were able to figure out what was happening. We had been at the lodge for a few hours now, and it was getting to be about twilight. The western-facing room we were in was painted yellow. The hall opposite from us was painted in a complementary shade of yellow and hosted a hall light with a golden-colored shade. The hall light was turned on, but the light in the room was not, as it was still light enough for me to take my notes by.

Thinking ourselves a clever bunch, we concluded that the setting sun coming through the window refracted the light and bounced it all around the yellow room. Then, when combined with the yellow light from the yellow hall, it produced a like-colored prism that seemingly floated in the room. With only this relatively sound scientific theory, we all felt very smart about ourselves for having cracked the mystery of the ghost flame in a house where there has never been a fire.

Until, that is, we spoke with Anita. Then we all felt rather sheepish. Apparently, when the paranormal investigators took the picture, it was closer to midnight than sunset.

We thanked the proprietress for her time and hospitality and were on our way. It was getting dark after all.

19

Vampire Beast of Greensboro

Crypto Zoological Mystery

> "The true mystery of the world is the visible, not the invisible."
> -- *Oscar Wilde (1854–1900)*

Isn't it always the case that something fantastic or supernatural happens and there is never a credible witness to be had? Not this time. Guildford County Commissioner Billy Yow filed the report himself. He lives over on the rural side of Greensboro and four of his goats were found dead on his property. The necks of the poor little things had been snapped and the blood had been drained from their body through what can only be described as bite marks.

Attacks like this are certainly reminiscent of what we imagine a vampire attack would be like—a lifeless body found drained of blood and the only sign of attack being the tell-tale puncture wounds on the neck. No one is sure what sort of creature caused the death of those goats, although many theories abound. But the simple fact of the matter is that this is not the first time this sort of attack has been reported in the area.

The first account came on December 29, 1953 and was reported to the authorities of Bladenboro, a sleepy little community surrounded by pine forests and swamps. Bladenboro is in the

Vampire Beast of Greensboro

southeastern edge of the Piedmont region, about 135 miles south of Greensboro. The farmer who actually made the report lived in Clarkton where the attack happened. He told local law enforcement that a large catlike creature had attacked one of his dogs and pulled it off into the underbrush.

A few days later, on New Years Eve, two dogs who belonged to Johnny Vause of Bladenboro were found ripped asunder, their bodies were described as having been "torn to ribbons and crushed." The police report that was filed also stated that their blood had been drained away. Two days after that, two additional dogs were found in a like manner. They had belonged to farm owner Woodie Storms. Other animals were also being targeted: goats, small cows, calves, and a couple of hogs. All the reports read the same—all the animals had their necks broken, their skulls and jaws crushed, and their blood drained away. Something was targeting the livestock of the area and police were not turning up any real clues as to the identity or motive of the killer.

Then came the report that authorities were most afraid to hear—that the beast had taken an interest in humans. The creature had chased a woman into her home, a young mother named Mrs. C. E. Kinlaw. Her husband Charles chased the animal off with his gun, and later found large paw prints all over his yard. The Beast was described as being about four or five feet long, around one hundred pounds, with dark brown fur, a round faced, shiny eyes, small round ears, a long tail, and a catlike face. Its cry was said to be blood-curdling, like a child or woman crying.

Police Chief Roy Fores led the hunt himself into the nearby four hundred-acre swamp looking for the creature. Mayor W. G. Fussell called the *Wilmington Morning Star* and reported this latest event to local paper. The front page of the January 5, 1954 edition read "Vampire Tendencies Found In Bladenboro's 'Monsters.'"

Mayor W. G. Fussell was later quoted as having said to *The Carolina Farmer* magazine back in 1958 that "a little publicity never hurt a small town." The Mayor also owned the Bladenboro movie theater, which by an amazing coincidence was showing a movie that was about an Alien Big Cat (also known as an *ABC*) roaming the English countryside.

Chapter Nineteen

A swarm of hunters, some reports claim as many as 1,000, came from far and wide. They descended upon the area, each one wanting to be the man who bagged what the papers had tagged as "the Vampire Beast of Bladenboro." The town didn't even have that many registered residents back then, in fact, it only has about 1,700 now. News of the Beast was carried in papers as far north as New York and as far west as Arizona.

Two weeks of chaos followed, hunters walking the woods with guns shooting at anything that moved. It was a small wonder that no one accidentally shot anyone else. It was said that even the best hunting dogs refused to follow the trail. However, the mysterious attacks had stopped and in an effort to return their town back to a sense of normalcy the Mayor and Sheriff took the body of an unusually large bobcat that had been killed, and literally ran it up a flagpole in the center of town. A sign posted below read "This is the Beast of Bladenboro." It took another week, but their plan worked, as the hunters slowly drifted back to where they had come from.

Now, fifty-four years later, dogs started to disappear in Bolivia, North Carolina, located in Brunswick County. A large catlike creature was witnessed in the area, and even a blurry photo was taken of it. Five dogs in all went missing, including two large pit bulls, which immediately ruled out the possibility of coyote attack in the minds of the local wildlife commission. The authorities came and looked into the matter as three-inch wide paw tracks and scat was found near the vicinity of the attacks, but nothing conclusive was ever reported. Remembering similar events from years ago, locals started calling the mysterious creature the "Beast of Bolivia."

One of the pit bulls was buried by its grieving owner about a quarter of a mile from his house. The next morning the still grieving owner was shocked and horrified to discover the body of his beloved dog back in his yard in the exact location it had been found dead in. Someone or something had apparently followed him to the gravesite, unburied the animal, and returned it to the location of its death. Why man or beast would do such a thing is beyond logic or reason.

Bolivia, North Carolina is a long way from Greensboro, about 225 miles. Bladenboro is also pretty far off, 135 miles. So why

Vampire Beast of Greensboro

worry? Because there are also reports of dogs and small farm animals that have gone missing or have been discovered with their heads crushed in and blood drained in Charlotte, about ninety miles away. And in Lexington, which is a mere thirty-five miles south. And did I mention that in the summer of 2004 a strange catlike animal was reported being seen in the Asheboro area, a short twenty miles from Greensboro. It was the same summer that numerous dogs went missing and it even drew the attention of the late Animal Planet star Steve Irwin, who had shown interest in coming to town to track the animal for himself.

And now, after what is apparently a slow but ever northwestward trek, County Commissioner Billy Yow's goats have been found with the blood drained from their bodies. I spoke briefly with Commissioner Yow about the attacks. His personal opinion about the creature that killed his goats is nothing at all related to the paranormal and even chuckled when I used the term "vampire cat." Yow feels that with all the building and development happening up in the mountains that the predators are moving off the mountain and into the area. He doesn't think that the creature is anything supernatural, but would not be too surprised to learn if it was a big cat hybrid of some sort. Yow has a stuffed and mounted forty-pound bobcat in his office.

So, is the Vampire Beast of Greensboro kin to the Beast of Bolivia and the Beast of Bladenboro? Or is it a more mundane animal, such as a bear, bobcat, coyote, cougar, or wild dog. Can it be a hybrid of any of the above mentioned? There are those who label it a Black Panther, Cryptid Felid, Mystery Cat, or Phantom Panther in lieu of having to say the words "vampire-cat."

I will say this much about the Vampire Beast—I believe that I saw it myself.

When I first moved to North Carolina in 1993, my husband and I rented a house with a fenced in yard in the town of Robbins, a small and rural community. I was talking on the phone to my husband's friend, Ben, when I heard my dog Clyde, a Belgian Malinois, barking up a storm. I had never heard him raise such a fuss or sound as vicious as he did then. My initial concern was that someone was hunting through my yard, and although I'm not opposed to hunting,

Chapter Nineteen

I am opposed to trespassers. As soon as I opened the back door, I saw Clyde right at the chain-link fence barking madly at a big cat not five feet away from him on the other side of the fence.

The big cat was sitting on its haunches and acting as if nothing in the world was happening around it. It could not care less that there was a very territorial dog daring it to take up on his challenge let alone me standing gap mouth with a phone in my hand. The big cat sat there lazily licking its front left paw, occasionally twitching its tail. It was darker than I thought a mountain lion should be, like the color of milk chocolate. It's ears, muzzle, and tail tip were darker. The paw it was licking was also dark, but I can't say if that was because it was wet or because that was the natural color of its fur.

It was a surreal experience. I was totally captivated watching this animal licking thoroughly its paw as it ignored the fact that my dog, could he get through the fence, would have unwisely attacked it.

When I was finally able to tear my eyes away from the scene, I told Ben what I was looking at. He taunted me for being a city girl and chided me for not being able to tell the difference between a feral cat and a mountain lion, a creature, he added, that was reported to be extinct in this area for over a hundred years. I stomped off to find my camera and remember bantering back and forth with him that if it was a house cat gone feral, it was bigger than my dog.

As is always the case, by the time I had returned with my camera I was just in time to see it saunter off into the thick woods behind the house. And the photo I took later revealed nothing but the thick brush.

When my husband came home from work that evening, I told him what I had seen. We called Ben over to the house and with Clyde leading the way we went to where I had seen the big cat. Sure enough, there were muddy prints, but too muddy to tell for certain what they were.

In Conclusion....

There are so many places in our country that boast and brag about their commercialized historical past. They lure you to the location, charge you an arm and leg merely to approach, and then surround the very thing you came to see with velvet ropes, not allowing you to complete the journey. Then, in the same breath that they tell you "no flash photography," they herd you through the exit cleverly disguised as a gift shop to buy their mass-produced prints for sale.

That's not the way it should be; that's not how to discover your roots or explore the past. I hope that you enjoyed my book and have now decided to swing by this way and see Historic Greensboro for yourself. If you do, I highly recommend taking a walking tour of the downtown area as well. The one that I personally endorse is Black Cat Tours, Inc. because I know that their year-round, ninety-minute walking tour is filled with historically accurate information about the city. Plus, it's fun weather you believe in ghosts or not.

Index

Alexander, Louise Brevard, 63
Allgood, Lucile Gray, 120
Arlen House, 62
Arlen, Love, 62
ArtQuest, 129
Asheboro, Randolph County, 129, 131, 155
Asheville, North Carolina, 32
Aycock Auditorium, 22, 25, 27
Aycock, Charles Brantley, 25
Aycock, Jane, 25

Battle Forest Apartments, 101, 102
Battle of Guilford Court House, 15, 21, 70,73, 97,101, 104, 108, 145
Battle of Yorktown, 17
Battlefield Avenue, 137
Beast of Bladenboro, 154, 155
Beast of Bolivia, 154
Beauregard, P. G. T., 44
Belk Brothers Company, 140
Best, Mary, 4, 93, 95, 96
Biltmore Hotel, the, 4, 18, 28, 32-38, 40
Bladenboro, North Carolina, 152-154
Bland, Charles, 41
Blandwood Plantation, 4, 41, 17, 42-45, 47
Blue Bell Hill, Kent, England, 116
Bogart's Hall Investment Co., 33
Bolivia, North Carolina, 154
Bonnlee Bennett Road, 89
Brown, Cynthia Moore, 4, 112
Bulwer, Edward Earl, 111
Bumpass-Troy House, 117

"Camp, Mary," 104
Card, Orson Scott, 21
Carolina Circle Mall, 19
Carolina Theatre, 28, 32, 48-60, 118
Carnegie, Andrew, 23
Carver, George Washington, 24
Castle McCulloch, 67-69, 158-159
Cedar Street, 61, 63
Celebration Station, 129
Charlotte, North Carolina, 155

Cheek, Joey, 21
Chestnut Street, 64, 65
Choir Room, the, 70, 71, 73
Clinton, Henry, 97, 98
Communist Worker's Party, 19
Cone, Bertha, 28
Cone, Betty, 56
Cone, Caesar, 17
Cone, Moses, 17, 28, 30, 38, 96
Cone Export and Commission Company, 30
Coolidge, Calvin, 53
Copper Creek, 67-69
Cornwallis, Charles E., 15, 98, 99, 101
Cox, Jacob Dolson, 44

Dan River, the, 99
Dana Auditorium, 4, 70-74
Davie Street, 15
Davis, Alexander Jackson, 43
Deep River Meeting Cemetery, 124
Deep River Mine Shaft, 67, 68, 87
Dennison, Ronnie, 4, 34, 36, 39, 40
Devil's Tramping Ground, the, 75-92, 145
Devil's Tramping Ground Road, 77, 90
Dix, Dorothea, 44
Downtown Revitalization Committee, 19
Dunleith House, 17
Durham, John, 4, 102, 106, 107

East Raleigh Street, 89
East Hendrix Street, 64
Elm Street, 15, 21, 140, 144
Emerald Pointe Water Park, 129
"Essie," 96

Farago, Karl, 150, 151
Fields, Lydia J., 111, 121, 122
First National Pictures, Incorporated, 48
Fischetti, Stephanie, 64-66
Fores, Roy, 153
Foster, J. H., 108
Four Seasons Town Centre, 19, 145, 147
Frey, Melba, 57, 60

Index

Friendly Avenue, 62, 74, 93, 95
Fullbright, James, 57, 58
Fussell, W. G., 153

Gainesborough, Thomas, 34
Gaston Street, 15
Gateway City, 8-11
Galey and Lord, 17
Gibson, Mel, 97
Gill, Anita, 145
Glendon Road, 89
Gray, Brian, 58, 60
Gray, R. T., 23
Great Road, the, 99
Greene, Nathanael, 15, 21, 99-101, 106-107, 145
Green Street, 15
Greene Street, 15
Greensboro, 4, 6, 8-13, 15-16, 18-19, 21-22, 24-25, 28, 30-33, 40, 43-44, 48, 53, 56, 59, 61-64, 68, 75, 89, 99, 102, 109, 112, 118, 122, 129, 136-138, 140, 142, 153-157
Greensboro Avenue, 89
Greensboro Children's Museum, 21, 129
Greensboro Coliseum, 19, 147
Greensboro Inn, 31
Greensboro Preservation Society, Inc., 44
Greensboro Triad area, 6
Greensborough 11, 15, 17-18, 21, 41
Greenwich Inn, 31-32
Grenadier Guard Apartments, 101
Guilford College, 70, 74
Guilford County, 21
Guilford County Department of Births and Deaths, 120
Guildford County Historic Park, 21
Guilford Courthouse National Military Park, 21

Harden, John, 145
Harden, John Jr., 146
Hardison, Burke, 117, 120
Harper's Crossroads, 88
Harris, Robert B., 24
Hayes, Richard, 82-89
Highlanders 71st Regiment, 105
High Point Road, 112-114, 117, 122, 145
Highway 64 East, 89
Historic Jamestown Society, 123
Hudak-Wise, Colleen, 4, 81
Humphries, Henry, 41, 43

Ice House Skating Rink, 21, 89
Irving, Washington, 129
Irwin, Steve, 116

"Jack," 155
Jamestown, North Carolina, 67-69, 109, 113, 122-123
"Jazz Singer, the," 53
John Motley Morehead Commission, 44
Johnson, Rhonda, 4, 70-71, 74

Keeley Institute, 44-45, 47
Kennedy, Jacqueline, 32
Kern, Milton, 33
Kersey, Elizer, 67
Kersey Valley Road, Jamestown, North Carolina, 69
King George, 97
Kingsway Tunel, Merseyside, England, 116
Kinlaw, Charles, 153
Kinlaw, C. E., 153
Klint, Petri, 116

"Largo," 53
Lee Jeans, 17
Levi Coffin House and Museum, 125
Levi Strauss and Company, 31
Lexington, North Carolina, 155
Lincoln Green Apartments, 101
Lorillard Tobacco Company, 19
Lydia's Bridge, 68, 79, 109, 111, 113-123

Macy's (department store), 33
Market Street, 18
Marlette, Dough, 21
Martin Luther King, Jr. Road, 89
McCulloch, Charles, 67
McCulloch Gold Mill, 67
McIver, Charles Duncan, 22-23
Mendenhall, James, 67, 123
Mendenhall, Mary Pegg, 124
Mendenhall, Minerva, 124-125, 128
Mendenhall, Richard, 125
Mendenhall Plantation, 4, 67, 113, 123, 125, 127-128
Miss Coffin, 108
Moon Room, the, 70-73
Morehead, John Motley, 17, 43
Morris, James I., 76
Moses Cone Memorial Hospital, 19

N2 Belchen Tunnel, Switzerland, 116
Natural Science Center of Greensboro, 129
New Garden Road, 74, 99, 137
North Carolina College for Women, 24
North Carolina College of Agriculture and Engineering, 24
North Carolina Department of Agriculture, 79, 81

159

Index

North Carolina Division of Water Quality in the Department of Environment and Natural Resources, 87
North Carolina State Zoological Park and Botanical Gardens, 129
North Second Street, 89

O. Henry, 21
O. Max Garner Award, 63

"Painter, Eve," 106-107
Panther Creek, 133
Paramount Pictures, Inc., 50
Pets-U-Love Dog Grooming, 61, 63
Piedmont Triad International, 21
Piney Grove Church Road, 89
Pisgah Covered Bridge, 88
Pisgah, North Carolina, 88
Poteat, Ashlee Crayton, 4, 45
Porter, William Sydney, 21
Proximity Manufacturing Company, 30, 31
Proximity Mill, 15, 30, 32, 38-39
Public Theaters, 50
Pullen, R. S., 23
Purgatory Mountain, 129, 131-134

Ragsdale Arrowhead Collection, 123
Ragsdale, William, 127
"Rebecca," 4, 141, 142-144
Richards, E. V., 48
Richfield Road, 135-139
Robbins, North Carolina, 155
Roosevelt, Eleanor, 24
Roosevelt, Theodore, 24
Route 1, Baltimore, Maryland, 116

Saenger, Abe, 48
Saenger, Julian, 48, 50
Saenger Theaters, Inc., 48
Salon Blu', 18, 140-144
"Samos, Theodore," 106
Schiffman's Jewelry, 140
Schofield, John, 44
Scott, J., 4, 147
Sears Roebuck and Company, 9, 140
Siler City, North Carolina, 75-78, 89, 90, 92
South Chapman Street, 61
South Elm, 140, 144
South Green Street, 60
Southern Railroad Underpass Bridge, 109-111, 122
Smithsonian Museum, 19
Snow, Helen, 118
Spring Garden Street, 120
Spring Street, 27, 62

State Normal and Industrial College, 24, 63
State Normal and Industrial School, 22, 24
Stokesdale, North Carolina, 33
Stonefield Winery, 33
Storms, Woodie, 153
Summit Avenue, 137
Sycamore Street, 15
Swisher, Jeffrey "JP," 4, 48

Tate Street, 27
"the Hunter," 132-134
Tucker, M. Ray, 82-83
Twin Lakes Lodge, 4, 145-151

United Arts Council, the, 56
University of North Carolina at Greensboro, 18, 22, 63
Uwharrie Mountains, 131

Vance, Zebulon B., 17, 44
Vanstory Clothing Company, 140
Vause, Johnny, 153
Vernon Building, 140-144
Vernon, Richard, 140
Vernon, Virginia, 140

"Walker, John," 103
Walnut Street, 121
Washington, George, 17, 24, 99
Washington Street, 40, 47
Weil, Emile, 50
Welborn, Richard, 4, 61-63
Wells, Orson, 116
West Market Street Methodist Church, 18
West Main Street in Jamestown, North Carolina, 69, 129
West Raleigh Street, 89
West Washington Street, 40, 47
Wilder, Thornton, 24
Wilmington, North Carolina, 76, 132
Wolfe, Rowan, 121
Women's College of the University of North Carolina, 24
Women's Suffrage Movement, 24, 63
Woolworth's, 19, 21, 24
Workman, James M., 50, 53
Wrangler Jeans, 15, 17
Wyatt, Perry, 4, 87, 92

Yow, Billy, 152, 155

Zenke, Otto, 32-33, 36